Energise

Energise

How to survive and prosper in the Age of Scarcity

EDDIE HOBBS

PENGUIN IRELAND

PENGUIN IRELAND

Published by the Penguin Group
Penguin Ireland, 25 St Stephen's Green, Dublin 2, Ireland
(a division of Penguin Books Ltd)
Penguin Books Ltd, 80 Strand, London WC2R 0RL, England
Penguin Group (USA) Inc., 375 Hudson Street, New York, New York 10014, USA
Penguin Group (Australia), 250 Camberwell Road, Camberwell, Victoria 3124, Australia
(a division of Pearson Australia Group Pty Ltd)
Penguin Group (Canada), 90 Eglinton Avenue East, Suite 700, Toronto, Ontario, Canada M4P 2Y3
(a division of Pearson Penguin Canada Inc.)
Penguin Books India Pvt Ltd, 11 Community Centre, Panchsheel Park, New Delhi – 110 017, India
Penguin Group (NZ), 67 Apollo Drive, Rosedale, North Shore 0632, New Zealand
(a division of Pearson New Zealand Ltd)
Penguin Books (South Africa) (Pty) Ltd, 24 Sturdee Avenue, Rosebank, Johannesburg 2196, South Africa

Penguin Books Ltd, Registered Offices: 80 Strand, London WC2R 0RL, England

www.penguin.com

First published 2010

1

Copyright © Eddie Hobbs, 2010

The moral right of the author has been asserted

Set in 11/14 pt Bembo Book MT Std
Typeset by TexTech International
Printed in Great Britain by Clays Ltd, St Ives plc

A CIP catalogue record for this book is available from the British Library

ISBN: 978–1–844–88230–4

www.greenpenguin.co.uk

Mixed Sources
Product group from well-managed
forests and other controlled sources
www.fsc.org Cert no. SA-COC-1592
© 1996 Forest Stewardship Council
FSC

Penguin Books is committed to a sustainable future
for our business, our readers and our planet.
The book in your hands is made from paper
certified by the Forest Stewardship Council.

Man has a poor understanding of life. He mistakes
knowledge for wisdom.
He tries to unveil the holy secrets of our father, the Great Spirit.
He attempts to impose his laws and ways on mother earth.
Even though he, himself, is part of nature he
chooses to disregard and ignore it.
But the laws of nature are far stronger than those of mankind.
Man must awake at last and learn to understand how
little time there remains
Before he will become the cause of his own downfall.
And he has so much to learn.
To learn to see with the heart.
He must learn to respect mother earth – she who has
given life to everything.
To our brothers and sisters, the animals and the plants,
To the rivers, the lakes, the oceans and the winds.
He must realise that this planet does not belong to him,
But that he has to care for and maintain the delicate balance of nature
For the sake of the wellbeing of our children and
of all future generations.
It is the duty of man to preserve the earth and the
creation of the Great Spirit
Mankind being but a grain of sand in the holy circle
which encloses all of life.

*White Cloud (Mahaska), Chief of the Iowa (1784–1834). Twenty-five years
after his death, white settlers in Pennsylvania drilled the world's first oil well.*

Contents

Figures

Tables

Abbreviations

AMEX	American Stock Exchange
API	American Petroleum Institute
ASPO	Association for the Study of Peak Oil and Gas
BRIC	Brazil, Russia, India and China
CIBC	Canadian Imperial Banking Corporation
CME	Chicago Mercantile Exchange
CPI	consumer price index
CRAB	Canada, Russia, Australia and Brazil
EIA	Energy Information Administration (US)
EROEI	energy return on energy invested
ETC	exchange-traded commodity
ETF	exchange-traded fund
GDP	gross domestic product
IEA	International Energy Agency
IPO	initial public offering
mbpd	million barrels per day
NASDAQ	National Association of Securities Dealers Automated Quotations (US)
NDP	National Development Plan
NYMEX	New York Mercantile Exchange
NYSE	New York Stock Exchange
OECD	Organisation for Economic Co-operation and Development
OPEC	Organisation of Petroleum Exporting Countries
P/E ratio	profit/earnings ratio

PLC	public limited company
UCITS	Undertaking for Collective Investment in Transferable Securities
UN IPCC	United Nations Intergovernmental Panel on Climate Change
UNFCCC	United Nations Framework Convention on Climate Change

Introduction

The natural resources of the planet, especially oil, are depleting. This depletion is happening on our watch and it is the single most important economic change since industrialisation. This conclusion rolled across me like a series of thunderclaps four years ago. Like many people, I'd come to accept conventional thinking that oil scarcity was just another scare story exaggerated by oddballs determined to send us back to an Amish lifestyle abundant in self-sufficiency and social cohesion, but with no electricity. My way of thinking was very cosy – it was also pretty stupid and it was very wrong.

Think about it. Just about everything we do is based on oil. Through the use of mechanisation, earth is used to turn oil into food to feed 6.5 billion people. The quadrupling of the world's population since 1900 directly correlates to increased oil production throughout the twentieth century. Oil is the lifeblood for our transport, pharmaceuticals and plastics industries, and just about every other product and service you care to think about. It is the world's most efficient, scalable, transportable source of energy, as well as being the safest.

A temporary disruption in oil supply can have game-changing economic consequences, as we learned during the oil crisis in the 1970s. A permanent depletion in oil supply – created by the rising gap between falling production and rising energy demand – won't just change economics, it will change society and how we live for ever.

The world endowment of recoverable oil has a limit. Individual oil fields have natural lifetimes from discovery to exhaustion, which is measured in decades. Peaking occurs when half the world's recoverable oil has been produced and depletion sets in. World peaking occurs when, even allowing for the addition of new fields, the overall production of oil still begins to decline. Supplies become scarcer and prices rise. In a society as dependent on oil as ours, that's a serious situation, and one that could be just around the corner.

You might, then, expect peak oil to be in the news every day. There are many reasons it isn't. The experts who estimate oil reserves use a range of technical tools, overlaid with a great deal of personal judgement, in their calculations and, even though they are using the same data, they arrive at different estimates for peak oil. Politics and commercial self-interest also play a role with oil-field owners exaggerating their reserves to gain business advantage and national governments relying almost exclusively on reports from the International Energy Agency (IEA) as a base for their national development strategies.

The IEA is a Paris-based organisation that advises most of the world's leading industrialised economies on energy use. Until 2008, IEA data was based on estimates supplied from markets rather than from an audit of world oil. However, in November of that year, following a detailed study of oil fields, the IEA dramatically shifted its position from being sceptical that a world peak would soon be reached to admitting that it could occur within the next two decades. In a report that shattered many of the myths about oil, the IEA doubled its estimate of decline rates from 3.7% per year to 6.7% per year, and now estimates that another four Saudi Arabias would be needed to plug the depletion rate in oil production over the next twenty years just to meet current energy demand. It would take six Saudi Arabias to meet demand if growth were to continue at its present rate.

In a landmark report to the US Department of Energy in October 2005, Robert Hirsch, a noted senior energy programme advisor who directed the US fusion energy project in the 1970s and who has managed technology programmes across most aspects of energy technology, warned that waiting until world peak oil occurred before taking action would lead to two decades of significant deficits in liquid fuels. He further estimated that even if a crash programme were initiated ten years before the peak was reached, there would still be a decade of fuel shortages. Only a crash programme that was begun twenty years before peak would avoid a world liquid fuel shortfall.

Peak oil for individual fields rarely becomes obvious until well after it has physically occurred, and it is then usually followed by rapid depletion. Global peak oil has been variously forecast by independent experts to occur sometime between 2005 and 2011. The IEA estimates that it will occur around 2030, but that estimate relies on dubious growth estimates of oil production from non-conventional sources such as Canadian oil sands and natural gas liquids. It also assumes there will be a huge investment in new infrastructure and that there will be continued co-operation from the oil-producing nations, many of whom are facing domestic peak oil and increasing domestic demand. By contrast, the Energy Watch Group, a Berlin-based independent scientific organisation, estimates peak oil occurred in 2006 and it challenges the IEA estimates of conventional world oil reserves being at 1.255 trillion barrels, instead placing them 32% lower at 854 billion barrels. Energy Watch Group says the biggest disparity is in the Middle East, where it estimates oil reserves are some 46% lower than the IEA figures. On Friday 13 November 2009 the *Guardian* newspaper reported on a senior IEA official spilling the beans about US pressure on the IEA to underplay the looming oil shortage in order to prevent panic buying. The official claimed that the IEA was understating the rate of decline and overstating the likelihood of new discoveries.

The economic crisis in 2008 pulled oil prices down to a little over $30 a barrel, providing temporary relief from the sky-high prices that had touched $147 a barrel a couple of months before the crash. But even as the global economy grappled with the impact of the banking crisis, oil prices began to rise again and crept past $60 a barrel in May 2009. While we may continue to experience shocks and reversals before real recovery begins, the recession doesn't change the underlying mismatch between oil production and growth in demand embedded in the global economy. The current recession has merely delayed the inevitable. At the time of writing in late 2009, it still isn't clear if emerging economic growth is going to be sustainable, especially in the USA, or if it is merely a stimulus-driven burst before another leg down into a multi-year depression. Such is the level of debt carried over from at least two decades of excessive borrowing for consumption purposes across the US consumer sector that government supports and incentives, such as cash for clunkers (a scrappage allowance for old, inefficient cars), may not prove to be adequate counter measures.

The real possibility remains of a long-term trend among US consumers to save and repair debt rather than to return to past consumption patterns, while inflation is exacerbated by the dollar going into freefall because of the yawning US deficit. What will happen to the world's leading economy, which accounts for 30% of global GDP and is 70% dependent on consumer spending, is anybody's guess. But the real story of oil is being driven by factors elsewhere, especially red-hot demand from fast-growing, non-OECD countries. (In simple terms the OECD is Europe, Japan and North America, and the non-OECD is just about everywhere else.)

A major global recession was avoided during the dotcom bubble burst from 2001 to 2003 because the Bush administration flooded the US economy with cash through a tax scheme and sharply lowered interest rates. However, arguably all this did was help fuel a credit bubble and buy time before the end of the long economic cycle that started in the early 1980s, bookending the high inflation of the 1970s, which was characterised by low interest rates, low inflation and largely uninterrupted growth. The big by-product of the age that started with Reaganomics was the creation of a globalised economy that put non-OECD economies on an unstoppable growth path and led to a scramble for the limited natural resources of the planet.

But what if the recessions of 2001–3 and 2007–9 are part of the same major adjustment, heralding the end of the latest economic era, whose death has been avoided artificially by a massive credit bubble? What if this latest adjustment announces the beginning of a new economic age? What if most of the wealth built up in the intervening years is no more than an illusion fuelled by excessive credit, and we're going back to where we were, just with less credit and tighter regulation? Or, worse, what if bigger forces are at play and we are entering an entirely new economic age: the Age of Scarcity?

I wrote *Energise* as a way of finding answers to these questions for myself and also as a warning to Irish, European and international readers. If my line of thinking is accurate, whether we face ruin or prosperity depends on how well we're prepared for the major structural shift that is already underway.

Let me tell you what I have found. In 2005, in the challenging Irish television series *Rip Off Republic*, I explored how energy operates in Ireland and why prices, interlinked with inflated property values, were so high. In the aftermath of *Rip Off Republic*, I set out to disprove the theory on peak oil, because I reckoned it couldn't stack up.

Peak anything is that theoretical point where half the easy-to-reach and cheap natural resources, like oil, have been consumed. It doesn't mean the end of supply, but it does mean the beginning of scarcity pricing as supply plateaus and demand rises above it. What I have learned from my research has not only alarmed me, but has changed my entire thinking about personal investment planning, about the global economy and about the environment. This journey took me through the pros and cons of what was then a narrow theoretical debate: that oil prices were set to escalate rapidly to well over $100 per barrel, that the fundamental value of oil was more likely to be as high as $500 a barrel and that a prolonged period of boom and bust linked to volatile price spikes in energy seemed unavoidable. The information was out there, and there was lots of it; all it needed was a willingness to look around the corner – and no great intellectual insights on my behalf because I have none.

In March 2006 I told a Progressive Democrats party gathering in Limerick to buy gold because the biggest risk to the Irish economy was a credit-bubble burst in the US. The audience pretty much ignored my advice and a Sunday newspaper sneered. The next year I urged the Green Party's pre-election conference in Galway to enter government but to switch their emphasis from climate change to oil scarcity. But even the Green Party, whose senior members know the energy story, stuck with CO_2 emissions and carbon taxes as the main course, despite the fact that the Irish economy is at an elevated risk of collapse until the country becomes energy independent.

In 2008 the government, which at this stage included the Green Party, issued two key reports on oil: one dealing with the security of supply and the other with the national plan to deal with shortages. Although more than forty risks, such as labour strikes, terrorist attacks, etc., were examined, neither report dealt with the most important national risk – a permanent decline in oil supply. In fact, in neither report was there even one sentence mentioning peak oil, despite the fact that, in the same year, the IEA, of which Ireland is a member, was conducting a game-changing audit on world oil reserves.

In the meantime, important events have intervened. In 2009 Spirit of Ireland – a private initiative by Irish entrepreneurs, academics and engineers – was launched in a series of national ads with the aim of making Ireland largely energy independent by utilising Ireland's unique Atlantic-facing topography and weather patterns to generate electricity from wind and hydropower. The organisation's exciting plan has been a breath of fresh air and has helped match Ireland's ephemeral and limited energy ambitions with a solid solution. At the very least, this plan has accelerated the important debate on Irish energy and, at best, it may play a pivotal role in the country's energy solution. Any ambition to transform the Irish economy into a net energy exporter and a beacon for foreign direct investment, attracted by long-term, reliable, low-carbon energy and price security, is worth pursuing.

Globally, the single most important event of recent years has been Barack Obama's election to the US presidency. Obama's chief medium-term goal is to wean the world's largest economy off Middle Eastern oil imports by 2020, a staggering ambition and one set to transform the USA. Listen closely to him and the US president puts energy as his top priority ahead of healthcare and education. Clearly, Obama gets it – and his leadership at this crossover may yet prove to be critical in raising energy to the top of the global economic agenda.

Between 2005 and the downturn in 2008, oil prices increased nearly threefold – and that is just the beginning. By mid-2008, the price of oil had raced past $100 per barrel and was touching $147. Then came the credit-bubble burst. In simple terms, the burst has eliminated most of the wealth accumulated during the five years since the dotcom bubble. But what it hasn't eliminated is the long-term mismatch between the growth in demand for energy and other natural resources and the level of production at current prices.

Originally dismissed as cranks, those few writing on these themes some years ago foresaw what was to come. I was a late convert. I admit I don't know how high oil prices will go or if some of the more extreme forecasts, like economic collapse, will come to pass, but I am now convinced that the old conventions of safe investment in traditional assets are going to prove very wrong and will destroy wealth as we enter a long period of high inflation. I am also convinced that the combination of peak oil and the need to transform the way we live and measure economic growth, coming at a time when human beings have created a global communications revolution, will spark a new revolution in invention and innovation in clean energy, in energy efficiency and in new sciences which will lead, after a period of turbulence, to a new age in human development in which we finally learn to switch from measuring progress narrowly by GDP to measuring progress by pricing it against the theft of resources from our children and their children.

However, for the moment, Ireland still sleeps. The destruction of tax revenues, which is crippling public finances, is not, as is commonly thought, the greatest challenge to Ireland's economic wellbeing. Far more serious is its energy dependence on imported fossil fuels. Even if the long-term target of 40% green energy is achieved, Ireland will still depend on imports for 60% of its energy. Sitting on the western edge of the European energy grid, with practically no energy sources of its own, Ireland has one of the most exposed economies to turbulence in oil and gas pricing in the world.

Even if the renewable energy targets set by the government are achieved, they will not be enough to stave off an energy drought and a sharp economic reversal caused by competitive advantage shifting to favour nations with the greatest energy independence. Don't expect Intel to stay when the Irish national grid becomes unstable. We are in a race to leave oil as fast as possible but there is not yet enough urgency or public debate on the hard choices that lie ahead, like fast-tracking new, strategic energy projects and considering nuclear electricity interconnectors – whether the voters like it or not. If Ireland is to complete a northwest European energy grid, combining with France and Britain, multiple interconnections will be required. So far, there is one interconnector in development to Wales. It is a simple statement of fact that fanciful notions of generating 40% of our electricity from the wind are not viable without the ability to offload seasonal excess, for example on windy summer nights; without interconnection, turbines will need to be shut down with huge losses to investors.

That Ireland's energy policy is confused is an understatement. The Irish Department of Communications, Energy and Natural Resources is stuck in the past relying on outdated and discredited IEA reports not just for energy supplies but for the entire foundation of Ireland's national development plan. Ireland is not alone: most other countries have based their national economic plans on discredited and outdated IEA assumptions about the future of affordable oil. That's why, for Irish readers, I suggest a course of action you can take to elevate energy-related investment from a personal to a national priority. At least you won't be toiling on entirely barren ground or on ground hogged by weak Green initiatives. On the opposition side, the Fine Gael policy think tank has a multifaceted strategy, labelled NewERA, to develop a national recovery agency by a reform and refocus of state companies. It includes important thinking on renewable energy and removing Irish dependence on imported fossil fuels.

Despite occasional breakouts in the mass media, the peak oil message has been swamped by shorter-term issues like collapsing property prices and economic reversal. Predictably, it will only be as rising oil prices hit ever higher psychological barriers – first there was $50 per barrel, then $100, next $200 – that the scale of the emergency facing us will be grasped. The climate change debate followed a similar pattern – as forecasts were replaced by evidence, the argument was more widely accepted. The next question is, can we react in time?

The slowness in realising the truth that is emerging from the tyranny of facts that dominate the peak oil debate is easy to understand; there is an overwhelming array of vested interests promoting disbelief about the depletion in fossil fuels. Enormous sums of money are invested on the notion that there is an abundance of cheap fossil-fuel energy, especially oil, available on the planet. These vested interests range from the military and infrastructure industries through to automobile manufacturers and airlines and the governments that they hold captive in mutually binding economic relationships that have existed for generations. Collectively, a doctrine of rejection has been established that will crumble only as oil hits super-high prices.

In Ireland, the get-out-of-jail card has been the National Development Plan. But it's a sham – the NDP is based on the falsehood that oil will be $100 per barrel by 2020, as enshrined in the government's 2006 energy policy. That, in turn, is based on an earlier IEA assumption that has already been proved wrong and which is challenged by the IEA's more recent reports (covered in Chapter 5). Ireland is building an infrastructure for an age – the cheap oil age – that has passed and is pricing the cost of the commodities and energy needed to implement the NDP on assumptions that are recklessly wrong.

Climate change and the damage caused by CO_2 emissions from fossil fuels are no longer regarded as quaint theories put forward by suit-and-sandal environmentalists, rather they are seen as very serious, real and current issues, as evidenced by the melting of the Greenland ice-cap and large ice fields in Antarctica. Oil depletion is following the same trajectory in terms of gaining widespread understanding but there's still a long way to go before the truth is accepted by the majority.

But you can act now. You can divest yourself of assets that will be hit hard by prolonged energy-led inflation and switch to assets that are positioned to create wealth during what will be the longest and largest commodity bull market in modern history. *Energise* will show you how to benefit. But you can also invest now in energy-efficient technologies ranging from basic cavity-wall injection to state-of-the-art smart meters and you can move from companies that make big-engined gas guzzlers to those pioneering smaller hybrid engines. There's a lot you can do to prepare.

While I am confident that human ingenuity, resources and technology will arrive to plug the gap between depleting oil and gas resources and rising demand, I've no confidence that these will arrive on time or at sufficient velocity to avoid a prolonged period, lasting between ten and twenty years, when we will experience a period of high inflation in both energy and commodity prices.

Not only does this pose significant problems to economies that, like Ireland's, are more exposed towards energy as an input cost, but it has the potential to devastate the balance sheets of those who are unwilling to prepare (for this reason Chapter 1 deals with the effects of the 1970s oil crisis). The best-case scenario is a turbulent few decades as we wean ourselves off oil while struggling with the gap between rising energy demand and affordable supply. The worst-case scenario is an economic collapse as we return to pre-oil age standards of living. Because this is a possible outcome if we reach a tipping point, having failed to make sufficient progress in reducing our dependency on fossil fuels, *Energise* will explore it.

Energise is delivered as a conversation, identifying along the way businesses that are interesting and appear, at least on a cursory glance, to be well positioned to benefit from the commodity bull market we are about to experience. But, be warned, I am not an expert in analysing individual companies and their share prices. I can identify economic trends and shifts and suggest how to allocate assets, especially into funds, but stock picking is a matter best conducted by experts. You will need to undertake more current research and, if necessary, take advice from suitably qualified stockbrokers and analysts who've freshly researched these companies, before investing. I have neither the skill, the experience nor the resources to do this. Instead, what I have done is select funds and exchange-traded funds (ETFs) as well as shares mostly in sector-dominant companies. Recent developments in ETFs and in exchange-traded commodities in Europe, especially by the investment group ETF Securities, provide a vast scope to play these markets without resorting to pure stock picking. This book will also introduce you to wild cards, more volatile embryonic companies that could have far higher upside potential, albeit with higher risks, to add some sizzle to your portfolio. You'll find these companies predominantly in the emerging green-energy sector, which still remains a minnow when measured against the breadth and scale of quoted stock markets.

The trick with any investing is to strike a balance that suits you. If you're uncomfortable with stocks, stick to funds. A well-managed fund or ETF will beat a poorly constructed stock portfolio hands down. However, if you like stocks, load up on sector-dominant players, but, at the same time, don't ignore the vast potential from emerging companies in green energy and, especially, in energy efficiency. Most Irish balance sheets are 50% to 70% dominated by Irish property and by Irish shares, whether directly held or through pension and investment funds. The common-or-garden variety mixed fund in Ireland has very little positive exposure to the mega-trends outlined in this book. This is why I've been urging diversification. There's no optimum mix of assets, but if your balance sheet ends up dotted with gold, energy, commodities and energy-efficiency investments added to index-linked Eurobonds and commercial property with rents linked to the consumer price index (CPI), to hedge against inflation, you'll have got the message and you'll be prepared for what is ahead.

Timing is everything and you should consider this book as a starting point for assembling a portfolio of investments that will help you benefit from the forces now unleashed. The downturn has compressed prices and earnings across all sectors, including energy, representing an opportunity to get into energy-related assets at values not seen for several years. In many instances prices by mid-2009 were at half their levels before the sharp downturn in equity markets, which represents a great opportunity to buy into some of the biggest energy and commodity companies in the world, companies that are sitting on a vast swathe of assets set to go sharply higher as demand growth regains momentum. In simple terms, for many fine companies 2001 prices are available in 2009. That doesn't make 2009 the ideal year to invest – far from it. By mid-year, it was already clear that very substantial risks remain to investors and that, as government-sponsored economic stimuli wear out, the global economy could go into another tail spin – in other words, a W-shaped recession. Remember, while the first shock to the banking system was delivered principally from sub-prime debt default, other shock waves lie ahead: for example, to refinance the credit market, large numbers of US borrowers will have to switch from their deeply discounted, adjustable-rate mortgages to higher-priced mortgages. Simultaneously, batches of commercial mortgages, which typically rollover every five years, are coming up for refinance in a difficult lending market as US commercial real-estate values continue to fall.

The rising cost of borrowing and lower property prices, combined with higher unemployment and bankruptcies, will act, at best, as a drag on US economic recovery, so vital to recovery elsewhere. The only good news about a protracted recovery is that it will give you time to prepare for what will happen afterwards when the global appetite for energy picks up pace again. But as the recovery begins, whether V-shaped, U-shaped or W-shaped, don't make the mistake of consigning the 2008–9 recession to history, filing it away as a banking crisis. Ask yourself, what fundamental conditions caused the crisis? Was it really just about sloppy regulation and greedy bankers chasing bonuses? Low oil prices and low inflation create low interest rates. Cheap borrowing accelerates credit expansion and pumps up speculative bubbles. Keep going for long enough and asset prices inflate across the board as credit becomes addictive – the only way to wealth is to leverage bank finance on those ever rising asset values as servicing the finance becomes easy because interest rates are so low.

But what happens when interest rates begin to rise as asset prices get red hot? What causes rates to go up? Take a close look at the recent history of recessions and most of them coincide with spikes in oil prices. In the run-up to the most recent recession, oil prices shot up sevenfold from a cosy $20 per barrel in 2000 to nearly

$150 per barrel by 2008. By 2007, US inflation, touching 6%, was being tracked by rising interest rates. The speculative bubble was about to burst and did so in dramatic fashion in 2008 when top US investment bank Lehman Bros collapsed under a mountain of debt. By 2009 interest rates had been cut to historic lows and governments had stepped in with massive stimulus packages. The evidence, by mid-2009, was that these steps had begun to stabilise the global economy, but even in the depths of the downturn, take a look at oil prices. After hitting a low just under $40 a barrel, prices had nearly doubled by the summer of 2009. What do you think will happen as the real recovery kicks in and oil demand rises? That's right, much higher prices and inflation. Oil isn't the only commodity to begin to race back, copper prices had also doubled by mid-year.

The first half of the book will take you through a basic understanding of commodities before presenting the evidence about why rising oil prices are not just a temporary glitch driven by speculation but rather a fundamental switch as the world moves past peak oil. If you're unfamiliar with the techniques needed to look under the bonnet of the financial data produced by PLCs, don't worry, I've transported and updated sections from my previous general investment book published in 2006 to help you prepare. Don't be put off by being introduced to new companies or the thought of buying shares directly. It's really quite simple, good companies exist all over the world, well positioned to grow while others fade. It's just a question of digging them out like truffles — and *Energise* provides a start for you.

Be prepared, you will be introduced to new lines of thinking that may significantly challenge your existing beliefs. Fund managers, life companies, major international investment houses and national governments continue to deny officially that there is an immediate and substantial problem with energy supplies at afford-able prices. The reason is simple. Accepting the problem would mean having to do something about it and face very substantial write-offs in the wealth buried in assets that are negatively exposed to the forces now at loose in the global economy.

That's why the book contains a full chapter on fresher information from the IEA released in November 2008 — and missed almost entirely by the media. The IEA report, and its interim warning that underinvestment in infrastructure during the downturn will lead to an imminent oil spike, is an early warning that these forces are already in play. So how can you prosper and avoid ruin in the coming Age of Scarcity? Well, let's start with what happened in the 1970s, a rough template for what's to come.

1. Learning from the 1970s

Why go into the past to learn something about what we face today? After all, if you look at any movie from the 1970s, you'll find rip-roaring, gas-guzzling V8 engines in the classic car chases that mimicked Steve McQueen's in *Bullitt* (1968). There was a big boom in North Sea oil production, as well as gas finds off Kinsale. Fashion was all over the gaff, but it was a time of the Bay City Rollers, Rory Gallagher and foreign suntans. Wasn't the 1970s a time of plenty?

If you're under forty today, you'll have no memory of the 1970s, but there was a prolonged energy crisis, triggered as a political response to the Palestinian–Israeli conflict, when Middle East oil exports to the US simply stopped during 1973–4. Heaven knows, I still go around the house turning off lamps, much to the annoyance of my wife who likes atmosphere, not because of these new energy-sensitive times but as a hangover from thirty-five years ago when electricity bills went ballistic and huge queues formed outside petrol stations throughout Ireland. I still hear my dad's voice echoing over the decades in between, '*Turn off the lights, turn off the lights!*' So there's much to learn from the 1970s, but this time around the solution won't be political. The fundamental problem isn't linked to an unresolved regional conflict but rather to an unavoidable global depletion of affordable oil.

Today's oil business started on the cusp of the American Civil War (which pitted the industrialised North against the slave-dependent South) when, in August 1859, Edwin L. Drake drilled down seventy-five feet on a farm in Pennsylvania and thus began the market for small, independent oil producers that John D. Rockefeller later consolidated to a near-monopoly with Standard Oil. The US remained the world's leading producer until its oil fields began to peak in 1970 at 11.3 million barrels of oil per day. However, the country's insatiable demand for oil to lubricate its vast suburban networks led the US to lose its energy independence and its position as the global price setter and to cede power to the Organisation of Petroleum Exporting Countries (OPEC) led by Saudi Arabia – a cessation that planted the seeds of the first oil crunch. By 1973, the Saudis had enormous surplus capacity at a time when worldwide oil dependency was sky high, having jumped from 19 million barrels per day in 1960 to 44 million by 1972, which is about half of today's demand.

The US rowed in behind Israel during the Yom Kippur War against Egypt and Syria, prompting Egypt's President Anwar Sadat to call for oil to be used as a weapon against Israel's allies. On 12 October 1973 OPEC demanded a doubling of its oil price and when Aramco, a combination of Western oil companies, stalled for time, OPEC's Persian Gulf members took control of the market, announcing that they would set the price thereafter. That October day, the day that the Israeli military gained advantage over the Golan Heights and the Sinai, Arab oil ministers announced an oil embargo to the USA and increased European prices by 70%. Although a UN-sponsored ceasefire ended the war on 22 October 1973, the OPEC embargo against the US remained until March 1974. The shock of OPEC's dominance on oil prices triggered a 15% fall in the US stock market in the first month of the embargo and a further 30% fall over the following year as US inflation climbed to as high as 12.8%. Industrial nations fell into the worst recession since the 1930s as high borrowing rates choked business expansion and house buying.

Just as the world was recovering from the events of 1973–4, the fall of the Shah of Iran to an Islamic revolutionary government led by Ayatollah Ruhollah Khomeini in 1979 pulled Iran from the oil market and underscored just how sensitive oil prices were to supply shocks. Iran produced 2.5 million barrels of oil per day, 5% of global supply. Its loss hiked prices by 150%, petrol queues returned and the price of a gallon of petrol jumped threefold. In the autumn of 1979, fifty-two hostages were taken by Iranian students at the US embassy in Teheran and held for more than a year, during which time Saddam Hussein of Iraq invaded Iran and severely damaged its oil fields and refineries. The Iran–Iraq War removed 8% of global oil supply, resulting in prices shooting up further.

The energy crisis of the 1970s led to stagflation, a combination of inflation (rising prices for consumers and businesses) and deflation (falling values for lots of businesses and assets) that flummoxed government decision making. Rising oil prices, leading to high inflation, cannot be cooled down by the traditional central bank reflex of raising interest rates, a method favoured by the European Central Bank. In essence, rising oil prices are like taxes. The money paid by consumers, after paying national taxes, flows to energy producers, distributors and service companies who make a bundle – as do their shareholders. Effectively there is a massive transfer of wealth from those negatively exposed to high energy-led inflation to those positioned to benefit from it. The extra cost of energy adds to the cost of everything and discourages business expansion. The result is a combination of high unemployment, high inflation and economic recession. The economy goes one way (downwards), prices go the other way (upwards), and consumers are squeezed in the middle.

The United States was the largest economy in the world in the 1970s, and self-sufficient in oil and gas, but even in the US unemployment doubled from 5% to 10% over a ten-year period.

As we exit the present recession, policy makers throughout the world will be faced with a difficult choice of either fighting inflation (but choking growth and exacerbating the risk of another recession) or stimulating growth by expanding government spending because businesses will be in retreat (but adding more fuel to the flames by pushing inflation to high double-digit levels). Unlike the 1970s, the difficulty this time is that the Anglo-Saxon economies, including the United States, the UK and Ireland, are hindered by debt. Raising interest rates to cool inflation in economies with high levels of government debt, corporate debt and personal debt could trigger a double-dip recession as borrowers become overwhelmed by rising debt costs. Such a step runs the risk of dipping economies back into contraction as money is diverted from buying goods and services into meeting higher debt repayments and higher energy costs. Faced with a choice of creating a depression – i.e. a multi-year recession – by raising interest rates and seriously curtailing the economy, the choice may be to let inflation run its course.

This raises the very real risk of hyperinflation in more exposed economies. Hyperinflation ravaged Germany after the 1919 Treaty of Versailles, Latin American economies in the 1980s, and the Zimbabwean economy in recent times. Under hyperinflation, prices soar out of control and money becomes practically worthless as a medium of exchange. The energy crisis of 1973–4 rocketed oil prices up tenfold, from $3 a barrel to over $35. Emergency rationing of oil occurred worldwide with people queuing outside filling stations for hours on end in order to get a limited allocation of petrol. Rising price inflation such as was seen in the 1970s, evidenced by increases in basic grocery items, radically changes consumer behaviour; consumers, fearing for their futures, switch from spending to saving while those on fixed incomes, or whose incomes fail to increase in line with rising workplace earnings, such as pensioners, become rapidly poorer each year when their pensions are not fully index-linked.

Inflation destroys wealth when badly exposed assets grow in value at a lower rate than inflation. Throughout the 1970s, in most economies, the average rate of inflation was higher than the return on government bonds and cash deposits, so the safest investments available lost considerable amounts of money. In general, equity portfolios crabbed sideways against inflation as they were made up of both companies that were negatively biased towards high energy-led inflation and those that were positively biased towards it. Companies raise their prices as inflation bites, making invest-ment in equities a good inflation hedge, but if your money is to grow it needs to be in companies that can experience real growth in their businesses, not just inflation growth. This is critical.

So how did investments in the strongest and largest economy in the world fare during the 1970s energy crisis?

The share prices for the largest US retailer in the 1970s, Kmart, commanded a beefy profit/earnings (P/E) ratio of more than twenty times earnings before the prolonged inflation cycle began in the early 1970s. (The P/E ratio is a classic measurement of how much the market is prepared to pay for a share. It expresses the share price as a multiple of the estimated earnings per share of a business.) Yet, despite growing its earnings by 17% a year for the next ten years, Kmart's P/E ratio dropped to single digits, ham-mering the value of shares in the USA's largest retailer.

What about investors holding Kmart shares for dividend income to support pensions? Even though Kmart paid dividends of 2% a year, US inflation ran 5% a year higher, so not only did its valua-tion fall fourfold, those still holding Kmart stock for its dividends lost money each year as dividends lagged price inflation.

So how do you avoid the Kmart effect? The trick is to invest in assets that have a positive bias towards inflation and avoid those that are negatively exposed.

There were three main periods of double-digit inflation in the USA during the 1900s, but the period 1974 to 1981 was the longest. Despite paying out average interest of 6.3% a year, US cash deposits delivered −10.5% in total, an average of −1.1% p.a. Remember, it is not the rate of return you get on the asset; it is the rate of return after you deduct the effect of inflation. *If you get 4% net of tax on an Irish bank deposit account but Irish inflation runs at 6% you lose 2% of your 'safe' money.*

The safest investments, US government bonds, returned 5.5% per year but still lagged inflation over the period at −17.5%, an average of −1.9% each year. General stock-market indices did not fare too well either. After inflation, the 500 largest PLCs in the USA tracked by financial analysts Standard & Poor's – the S&P 500 – produced −14%, that's a yearly average of −1.5%, even though the nominal rate of return on the S&P 500 was 5.9% p.a.

Undifferentiated general indices, like the S&P 500, that track companies purely on the basis of size contain companies that will lose money heavily due to high energy input costs, such as airlines. This is particularly the case for the highly popular index-tracking funds introduced in Ireland in recent years by firms such as New Ireland, Irish Life and Quinn Life. The same weakness holds true for uninformed but populist notions such as buying the Irish top ten stocks as the best strategy. These are simple but dangerous tactics promoted by those who favour putting lower management costs above all else, including human intelligence and stock picking. In 2007 to 2008, the devastating fall in the Irish stock market, which was so heavily reliant on Irish property through its dominance by banking stocks, underlines the folly of following approaches to growing wealth that rule out using human reasoning and ignoring major economic shifts.

Remember, when inflation rises, the P/E ratios across lots of businesses decline. High inflation reduces business confidence and curtails growth plans. Investors reassess value and look for lower prices, i.e. lower P/E ratios. Earnings growth is split into two elements – real growth, which comes from business growth, and inflationary growth, which is merely the impact of rising prices coming through into rising costs. When investors sense that most earnings growth is inflationary growth, they downgrade how much they are prepared to pay for stocks.

Certain sectors are more affected by high inflation than others. In the 1970s, traditionally defensive sectors, such as US cosmetics, retail stores and foods, fared badly, generating returns of -45%, -34% and -6%, respectively, when measured against inflation. Worst affected were industries that were exposed to high energy input costs: airlines shed -37%, chemicals -47% and automobiles -55%.

The economic growth of India, China, Brazil and Russia will also be affected by inflation. This is already evident. However, and notwithstanding the economic, social and political disturbance caused by rising prices, especially for food, most of the world's economic growth will still take place in these regions in the years ahead. Therefore, investing exclusively in big European and US companies whose earnings are over reliant on local markets won't be enough to beat inflation. Instead, you need to add to your shopping list large-capitalisation businesses that have good exposure to growth in these developing regions, and in India and China in particular. Investing in small companies with no developing market exposure, unless they have a strong energy story, is unlikely to produce good results.

It's a challenge to look past the current economic turmoil, rising public finance deficits, ultra-low interest rates and falling prices in certain sectors, and to consider what will follow – but that's what must be done. Nobody can say with any great certainty how long this recession will last or how robust or weak the subsequent recovery will be. All we can rely on is that the global economy will continue to function and that governments and financiers will work to return to an era of higher economic growth.

That growth cannot happen without a corresponding increase in energy demand, beginning the Age of Scarcity.

Ireland in the 1970s

In the world we live in today, you can choose to invest just about anywhere on the planet. This wasn't the case in the 1970s when exchange controls and other rules in many countries, including Ireland, limited the amount of money that could be invested abroad, restricting investor choice to local assets. The return on Irish assets in the 1970s reflected what was happening in the US and elsewhere but was even more severe.

From 1970 to 1979 the return on Irish gilts (bonds) lagged inflation by 5.2% per year, devastating the value of bonds in real terms by 40% over the period. Cash was nearly as bad, underperforming inflation by 3.1% per year, which meant that money held in top deposits lost over a quarter of its purchasing power during the 1970s. At the same time, Irish property, which would wait until the 1990s to hit a purple patch, produced negative returns of 2.6% per year below inflation. Irish equities just managed to hold their real value at 0.5% per year above inflation.

What followed in the 1980s was a boom in asset prices as inflation fell away and gold prices collapsed. Irish gilts returned 9.5% per year above inflation, cash 4.1% and equities 14% per year. Property returned just 1.5% per year above inflation, but a decade later it was returning a beefy 12.5% per year, outperforming equities (then at 11.8%) by the turn of the millennium.

The price slump didn't kick in until 2006, the peak of the credit bubble, and property prices are likely to continue falling for several years yet – if Ireland's bust follows the pattern of most busts in OECD countries since 1973, as outlined in UCD Economics Professor Morgan Kelly's excellent paper 'On the Likely Extent of Falls in Irish House Prices', published in April 2007 just a few weeks before the Taoiseach Bertie Ahern suggested that critics of the Irish economic model should consider suicide.

All that glitters when inflation runs high

Gold is a crucial hedge against inflation. Investors, spooked by negative returns from cash deposits and bonds and losing confidence in the value of currencies, are arriving in large numbers and triggering a bull market for gold as the ultimate store of value. It's easy to see why. The total amount of gold held in reserve worldwide is estimated to fill just four Olympic-size swimming pools – no wonder the yellow stuff has been the favoured ultimate currency since the time of Croesus.

During the 1970s, gold prices took off, with the average return on gold bullion over the period outperforming US inflation by 25.7% a year, producing a total return in excess of 880%. Before the recent turbulence in equity markets, all the gold in the world, approximately 200,000 tons, was worth about 25% of the value of the S&P 500. When gold reached its previous peak in 1980, it was worth $5.5 trillion, about five times the value of the S&P 500.

The oil companies make a killing, right?

In the 1970s, the major US-quoted oil companies produced an average rate of return of 14.2% a year, or 6.8% a year above inflation, leading to a total return of over 93%, but oil-service companies such as drillers did even better with an average return of 31% a year or 23.6% a year above inflation, a total return of 732% over the period! However, be careful: this time around, the big oil companies aren't so big and are getting squeezed by national oil companies. Oil service companies, however, are better positioned.

So what about an Irish addiction – property?

For property addicts there's good news, once prices finally bottom out. Rising inflation reduces the real value of outstanding debt, making bank-financed property investments attractive, whether through funds or directly, as favoured by the Irish. The average return on US real estate was 10.1% a year during the most recent high-inflation cycle, about 2.7% a year above inflation. But because of lousy economic conditions, Irish property fared much worse and did not start producing strongly positive returns above inflation until the 1990s. Much like any other sector, investment in property needs to be carefully made, ideally concentrating on geared property investment schemes where there is little risk that tenants will leave. Remember, high inflation will be characterised by rising unemployment and economic black spots. The safest property market to be in is in the best locations with strongly rated tenants guaranteeing good cash flows to meet borrowing costs.

I would recommend the German commercial property market

for three reasons: firstly, because it has not experienced a property bubble like Ireland; secondly, because it's a eurozone country, hence there's no exchange-rate risk; and, thirdly, because rents are linked to German inflation indices by way of market practice. Consequently, if you can lock into rental yields higher than fixed borrowing rates, you can let inflation do its magic, increasing rents each year. The least safe part of any property market is residential property in locations where there is high unemployment and long-vacancy risk. But except for ultra high net-worth private investors, multimillion deals in the commercial property market can only be accessed by investing in syndicates or funds for which there is a thriving market. Alternatively, small investors can choose to invest in large property PLCs through stock exchanges or through ETFs such as the EPRA Eurozone Property Index, which tracks thirty of Euroland's largest property PLCs.

Beware of long-term guarantees

Investments that provide future capital guarantees perform badly at times of high inflation. This includes tracker bonds in particular. These fashionable structured investment products guarantee your starting capital typically over periods of up to six years, but they do so by locking large parts of your capital into a deposit account and by buying options on shares with the rest. Options are like bets on a horse, you don't own the horse but if it comes in you can multiply your money. Ignoring the questionable nature of these options, future capital guarantees, which lock away your money at a period of high inflation, can have a devastating effect on the real value of your wealth. For example, a financial product that returned only your guaranteed capital investment after ten years during which inflation ran at 9% per annum would lose you 58% of your money: the €100 you invested in year 1 would be worth just €42 in real terms by the time you got it back.

Energise will introduce you to new investments, but no discussion on investments can be complete without a few timely if well-weathered warnings.

When you're told that past performance is no guide to future performance, you'd better believe it – it's not. Just because an asset, fund or a stock has performed well in the past or has behaved in a certain way under certain conditions is no guarantee that it will do the same in the future.

It makes sense to have a diversified mix of uncorrelated assets. In other words, put your eggs in several baskets. However, as *Energise* points out, all assets held should be screened for their positive or negative sensitivity towards energy-led inflation. I've said that certain assets like cash deposits and bonds do not fare well under the present conditions. This does not mean that you should not hold money in them but rather that you should use them as a way of holding money in the short term and not as major assets through which to build wealth as we head into a high-inflationary period. The only exceptions and an ideal long-term holding are index-linked Eurobonds, because the coupons paid by the issuing government are linked to inflation and as inflation looms, increased demand for the limited number of indexed Eurobonds will increase their capital values. Eurobonds are available through specialist funds.

Energise will introduce you to a large number of companies that you have probably never heard of before. This is purely an introduction. Investing your money in shares is not a decision that should be made quickly or on the basis of limited information. It is also important to get your timing right. The information provided in this book on companies should be seen as a starting point, not a blueprint. If you feel more comfortable passing the responsibility of stock selection to professionals, do so by all means. There are lots of good funds that will get you the sector exposure you'd like.

All experienced investors were novices once. If you're starting from scratch, don't worry, there's not much in *Energise* that's beyond a beginner. In truth, beginners have the advantage of coming at these challenging concepts and new ways of investing without the baggage of existing holdings and desperately hoping that *Energise*'s predictions will be wrong.

Many of the businesses identified in *Energise* are very substantial, large-capitalisation companies that have been around for generations and, as market leaders, are well positioned in the current climate. But even these stocks can be volatile and can be overwhelmed by unpredictable events. You will also be introduced to smaller companies that, with lower nominal stock prices, have explosive potential on the upside – but also on the downside, which means you could lose heavily.

Small capitalisation companies that are successful produce spectacular returns for investors. Those that don't make the breakthrough from their early-state development go into administration or go bust. In other words, if you invest in these companies, you could lose all the money you have invested. Remember, having a good spread and not over-concentrating on any one company, especially a small company, is important to protect the value of your balance sheet.

In *Energise*, each company named is accompanied by its ticker symbol and one of the stock exchanges where its shares are quoted, e.g. **Petrobras (NYSE: PBR)**. You can get a brief snapshot of these companies on websites such as www.reuters.com. Look for quotes and enter either the company name or symbol. Specialist companies such as ETF Securities (www.etfsecurities.com) provide substantial information on their websites about their exchange-traded funds and exchange-traded commodities (ETCs), including details of past performance and prospectuses. Each ETF or ETC will have its own stock-market ticker that you should use when giving buy or sell instructions to a stockbroker, ideally an online stockbroker, for example TD Waterhouse (www.tdwater house.co.uk), which charges a small flat-rate fee per trade.

The yawning gap between oil supply and demand isn't going to be filled quickly. It will take a lot longer than ten years to fix, but let's be optimistic that eventually sufficient capital and human ingenuity will arrive to turn things around. At that point, you must be prepared to sell your high-inflation position and get out into heavily underperforming assets that are likely to experience the next boom. Remember, even though they were hammered throughout the 1970s, bonds, cash and large parts of equity markets hit a long purple patch during the 1980s with equities producing the longest uninterrupted bull run in modern times.

So dust yourself down now and let's get going into the greatest opportunity to make money since Cortés met the Aztecs.

2. Myths

Nothing will convince a man more strongly to reject an idea if his balance sheet, his wealth and his income are dependent on believing the opposite. That's why myths come in handy in rejecting peak oil. You'll hear these at dinner parties and during economic and political discussions on TV but, unhappily, the doctrine of those in denial doesn't stand up to much challenge.

There's oodles of oil

Perhaps the greatest myth has been the notion that the world has a limitless supply of fossil fuel, including oil, and it is simply a question of going out and getting it. The contention that there's abundant oil is highly questionable, as we'll see later, but even if it were the case, it ignores a number of harsh truths. The first is that, although there are certainly untapped reserves of oil on the planet, the means to retrieve it simply aren't there in sufficient scale and will not arrive soon enough to avoid a yawning gap opening up between burgeoning demand on the one side and insufficient supply on the other. So, even if we accept that new oil fields, such as the recent finds in Iran, Uganda and the Gulf of Mexico, can be discovered and tapped, the oil will simply not arrive in time.

Secondly, the International Energy Agency, a traditional rejectionist of the peak oil proposition, is now admitting that there will be substantial tension between rising demand and the size of the oil tap until 2015 owing to underinvestment in infrastructure and new fields. But if we look into the detail of the latest IEA report on global energy trends, it's pretty clear that oil, if it hasn't peaked already, will do so in the very near future. But whatever the debate on the precise year of peaking, one thing that all sides are agreed on is that the age of cheap oil is well and truly over.

Thirdly, world crude-oil production hasn't increased in the past four years, according to Jeffrey Rubin, the former chief economist at Canadian Imperial Banking Corporation (CIBC), World Markets, but what has increased is the production of natural gas derivatives like propane and butane, which are typically in abundance as oil fields pass maturity and which are often misleadingly included in overall oil-field productivity figures. Non-OPEC producers such as Russia, Norway, Britain and Mexico peaked in 2004 and are now seeing big declines in crude-oil production. Saudi Arabia peaked in 2005. Increased OPEC production is not expected to be able to offset non-OPEC decline for long, perhaps just a year or two, and the pre-recession 2008 production figure of 73.78 mbpd (million barrels per day) is likely to have been the high-water mark for crude-oil production. Production of natural gas liquids, heralded as the saviour for energy markets, has stagnated, failing to exceed 8 mbpd over the past three years. Biofuel production is growing, but it is unlikely to reverse the decline. Brazilian and US ethanol production touched 1 mbpd in 2008, bringing total global biofuels to 1.5 mbpd.

There are lots of future liquid-fuel sources but, even combined, these are highly unlikely to make up for the decline from existing fields. It is thought that Arctic energy resources, mostly gas, will produce about 3 mbpd, but these won't be available for many years. The promising Santos Basin off Brazil could hold as much as 15 billion barrels, but it is in very early stages of development and by the time it comes on stream will probably be used to offset Brazil's declines elsewhere, adding no net gain to oil trading.

Canada's huge oil sands are often introduced as the get-out-of-jail card, but most of the oil they contain is both expensive and very difficult to extract. Producing oil from oil sands burns up huge amounts of gas and water, reducing the oil's net energy value. The estimated 165 billion barrels of oil available in Canada's oil sands is nowhere near as valuable as 165 billion barrels of untapped crude oil from a conventional oil field would be. Oil-sand production was 1.2 mbpd in 2007 and is forecast by the IEA to be 1.34 mbpd in 2009. Experts estimate maximum production from Canadian oil sands to be about 2.5 mbpd.

Iraqi oil is the most promising option. Previous underinvestment and the effects of recent conflicts can be countered with large-scale investment, new legislation and peace. Even so, Iraq is unlikely to reach more than 4 mbpd by 2014 and peak at 8 mbpd by 2020, which will be too little, too late.

Big money will arrive to get more oil

In greed we trust. Classically trained economists love the idea that the answer to all our problems is to be found in the lure of profit, but unfortunately this idea ignores two fundamental equations in relation to oil.

Firstly, it is assumed that just because we have the dosh, the oil will follow. This ignores geology. Despite the clear profit incentive, annual discoveries of new oil have been declining since the 1960s and, since 1984, the oil being consumed has exceeded the oil being discovered, an imbalance that cannot last indefinitely.

Secondly, if it costs more to produce something than can be

earned from selling it, you'd be nuts to invest in it. This is the second biggest flaw in the myth of abundant fossil fuels – it ignores **energy return on energy invested** (EROEI). Self-evidently, energy needs to be burned in order to do the job of producing new energy. As energy costs rise, the EROEI is depressed, but remember energy input costs aren't the only costs. It makes no sense to undertake energy production unless the return on the investment, which includes all costs including labour, energy, plant and equipment etc., is greater than one to one, otherwise there is no profit. More mature oil fields require higher amounts of energy to keep the oil flowing. More water or gases need to be pumped in to maintain field pressure. That costs money. Then there's the huge expenditure on pipes, people, transport, refining and shipping – all of which are dependent on oil and all of which will be affected by rising energy input costs.

Analysts examining investments estimate that any new energy business doesn't make sense unless the return on capital is at least five to one, to allow for the costs of infrastructure, management, etc. But profit comes under significant stress as oil prices rise, because it increases the energy input costs on one side of the equation and, while it also increases the price which can be obtained from the new energy created, the financing of the time gap between expenditure and delivery increases costs and risks.

Don't worry, oil is replenishing!

Abiotic oil theory proposes that oil isn't a fossil fuel at all but is, instead, formed by a non-organic process in the carbon deposits deep within the earth; hence, oil taken out of the ground is actually being reformed. This very handy theory has been knocking around since the 1950s but has very little evidence to support it and is discounted by most geologists. However, don't be surprised if it's dusted down and polished when oil prices sky rocket to explain that it's really just a temporary phenomenon. You can safely file this one with the likelihood of aliens landing a spaceship in the Phoenix Park, avoiding getting mugged and delivering to us the engineering codes to a new form of energy.

Rising prices will attract new players

Classically trained economists argue that as prices rise more profits will be made, which will attract more players, thus increasing production and meeting consumer demand. This is a constant theme in oil debates. It ignores the geology of non-renewable energy sources and is based instead on the crazy idea that as long as people are prepared to pay the price, the goods will be produced. Just because we are prepared to pay more doesn't mean that an angel will magic up more oil for us, regardless of how economists are trained to think.

We've enough oil for 100 years – what's all the fuss about 'peak'?

Sure we've even got oil that will stay in the ground for ever. But the key to understanding peak oil is to recognise what 'peak' actually means: the point where we've consumed half the available oil. Moreover, we've consumed the most easily available, highest-quality half from elephant fields, leaving the remaining half in hard-to-access places like deep-sea locations, or in widely scattered small fields that produce poorer quality crude. So the half we have left will require increasingly more energy to extract. And when the point is reached where it costs a barrel of oil to produce a barrel of oil, the exercise will become futile and whatever oil is left in the ground will remain there.

The estimated world endowment of oil when we hit peak is about 1,000 billion barrels. Some analysts, including Princeton geologist Ken Deffeyes, believe peak has already occurred – in 2001; others, including Dr Colin Campbell, the founder of the Association for the Study of Peak Oil and Gas (ASPO), reckon we got there in 2005. At current rates of demand, which is running at about 30 billion barrels per year, we'd be at *end* oil in less than forty years – and, considering rising demand from economic behemoths like China, it may be a lot sooner. Still, agencies like the IEA and other oil proponents have been determined to reject peak oil, counting on the potential reserves from untapped locations to satisfy world addiction to oil for a lot longer. The IEA has at least conceded that peak oil is foreseeable, but its estimated date of 2030 relies on untapped reserves coming on stream and on massive global investment in both maintaining and expanding oil and gas infrastructure. The gap between the 'peakers' and the IEA is explored further in Chapter 5.

Some climatologists and environmentalists support the notion of abundant fossil fuels. They are wedded to the struggle to convince national governments to adopt stricter emission targets and find that the notion of peak oil conflicts with their objectives. After all, if we face imminent oil depletion then, as we pass peak, CO_2 emissions will automatically decline and global warming pressures will be alleviated. Most peakers come from economic, analytical and scientific backgrounds and, it can be argued, are less concerned with the environment and more concerned about economic collapse and self-preservation.

Peakers take a pessimistic view of oil-production data, advocating that we're already past or very close to peak, whereas organisations like the IEA and the US Energy Information Administration (EIA), as well as companies like ExxonMobil, make very optimistic forecasts. ExxonMobil has been particularly active in undermining the peakers with adverts and PR proclaiming peak oil theory as flawed, a position now looking foolish following the most recent IEA report. Unhappily, the peakers have usually been proved right. As early as the 1950s, Marion King Hubbert, the original peaker, forecast US peak oil around 1970. The US Geological Society forecast it for 2000. US oil hit its peak in 1970 and reserves have been declining ever since, despite new finds. In 2001 the EIA estimated that British North Sea oil would reach peak in 2005, rising to 3.1 mbpd and declining to 2.7 mbpd by 2020. In practice, North Sea oil hit peak in 2003, at 2.684 mbpd, and had declined to less than 1.7 mbpd by 2005.

This time it's different – we're less oil dependent than in the 1970s

It's absolutely the case that, today, we burn a lot less oil per euro of GDP than we did in the 1970s oil crisis, but to confuse that with being less oil dependent is incorrect. We are even more oil dependent because we use a lot more oil.

Ask yourself, what happens when you add another lane to a motorway? There is a temporary gain but, eventually, more cars fill up the space created. Now consider oil. Huge gains in energy efficiency and lower prices encourage consumers to use more energy because they can afford it. Big energy efficiency drives in OECD countries that helped initially to lower the price of oil will simply encourage more energy demand in non-OECD countries. Cheap energy helps economies to grow and economic growth demands more energy.

Look around and ask yourself how many more items you now own that demand energy compared with, say, twenty years ago. Mobile phone chargers, PlayStations, computers, spotlights, a second or third car, iPods, flat-screen TVs – the list goes on. This economic behaviour is not unique. The invention of the steam engine by James Watt was unquestionably a huge leap forward in energy efficiency in the industrial age, but what happened to coal consumption? British economist William Stanley Jevons noted that, while coal demand initially fell, it proceeded to grow tenfold in the three decades following Watt's invention.

In short, initial efficiency gains have been outpaced by more energy usage. What have improvements in energy efficiency for cars and cheap oil led to over the past thirty years? There are far more cars on the road using more fuel. What about air travel? Huge improvements in aircraft design and engines that require less jet fuel per mile combined with cheap oil created a massive increase in low-cost airline travel. Gains in home insulation and construction technology have encouraged the building of bigger houses filled with many more energy-dependent items. Face it: so far, we've applied energy efficiency gains to simply do more things, not less. Energy conservation can't happen if energy prices fall, otherwise we spend the gain in higher energy consumption. This time around, however, it's different. Gains in energy efficiency are likely to offset – but not reverse – energy price rises, because the main source of energy, conventional crude oil, is depleting.

Those who hold on to the view that we are economically less dependent on oil than we were in the 1970s are kidding themselves. We may have learned the trick of how to do more with less oil, but that hasn't translated to using less oil. The gain has been spent on using even more oil and our lifestyles are even more dependent on oil.

Only a few lunatics believe this stuff

The fact is that no Western government is jumping up and down about the short window of opportunity available to wean the world off fossil-fuel dependency. Peakers remain a tiny minority among analysts, engineers and scientists. Everybody else disagrees, disregards or just completely ignores peak oil. Perhaps the reason that oil depletion is so difficult to accept isn't just a function of logic but has lots to do with human psychology. An imminent historic shift from cheap and abundant fossil fuels to expensive and scarce ones will affect just about everybody on the planet and everything we do. We are engineered to fight or flee from danger, but we respond sluggishly to dangers that are systemic and hard to personalise.

Just look at the recent systemic crisis in banking and consider the phases that occurred before action was finally taken: denial, anger, despair, acceptance, solution-seeking and, only then, action. In the case of the banking crisis, the evidence mounted over a two-year period. It took the Lehman Bros collapse in September 2008 to galvanise global action, but this tipping point was preceded by problems with Northern Rock a year earlier, with Bear Stearns, with Countrywide and with several other institutions. In early 2008 we were told that solving the banking problem would cost $40 billion, then we were told it would be $100 billion and then they said, OK, $300 billion tops. We were also told the problems would be contained within the banking system and would not cause a contagion in the real economy. These conclusions were

39

promulgated by the best brains and leaders in economics and banking and the best expert advisors available to national governments. They were all wrong. Why? Maybe because accepting the scale of the banking bust and its global consequences was just too big to contemplate and the hard evidence had yet to arrive – people need to put their finger in the wound before they can accept overwhelming change.

Oil depletion will follow a similar path before the reality gains widespread acceptance. Most people will simply not accept the evidence until it becomes personal – when oil supply reaches its tipping point. Self-evidently, accepting imminent fossil-fuel depletion requires establishing an international energy depletion protocol and a phased movement into a new world characterised by much lower energy usage and some revolutionary inventions. This would also pose very serious challenges, not least of which would be a switch from measuring performance purely in terms of traditional economics to sustainable economics and a switch from competing against future generations to supporting them. The impact on many businesses that are based on promoting unrestricted consumer demand for ever more stuff would be profound and a long period of economic contraction could begin.

If solutions aren't found, society may need to change – much like the change Cuba had to undergo when the Soviet Union collapsed in the early 1990s, switching from a heavily industrialised and fuel-dependent agricultural system to localised, labour-intensive farming. Consider the world's largest energy user, the USA, which applies 17% of its annual energy to agriculture and where food travels on average over 1,000 miles from farm to fork. It's estimated that 350 gallons of oil equivalents are needed to feed each American annually – in other words, every calorie of food requires eight calories of fossil fuel.

The US farming population has declined dramatically as a result of industrialisation and improvements in agricultural technology. The average age of a US farmer is close to 60 years, so who will grow the food in the event of energy disruption? In 1900, nearly 40% of the US population was involved in agriculture; today, it's about 1%. On those numbers, the US would need another 40 million farmers to make up for an energy decline. Just before the American Civil War, when the US agri-economy still outweighed its industrial economy, two-thirds of physical labour came from mules, horses and oxen, but today agricultural effort is almost entirely based on oil and gas. Ireland would be in better shape because of its food surpluses and its low population density, but it has also experienced a sharp decline in numbers engaged in agriculture as mechanisation and technology have advanced, and it too has an ageing farming population. But with little by way of national energy assets, the Irish food supply chain is hugely exposed to disruption in international energy markets.

In societies weaned on the economics of personal acquisition and individualism and wherever rising consumer demand is stoked by businesses seeking more growth, how do you implement phased economic transition to a less complex but more sustainable global economy? What politician wants to break the news that we need to embark collectively on a new direction, one that involves prolonged economic contraction? Oil is the king commodity that affects just about everything else, but look closely and other natural resources face huge strains and are close to peak. The list includes fresh water, uranium and high-grade coal. Many of the world's fish stocks are facing rapid depletion as we continue to absorb the global supply of natural resources without pricing in the cost of sustainability.

These are really hard questions, arguably harder than those central to the climate change debate because they're very personal, especially the question of energy consumption. Yet we intuitively understand that we're in an unsustainable self-reinforcing feedback loop. Higher energy demand leads to ever higher fossil-fuel mining that creates ever more energy demand.

Fail to plan and you plan to fail

One thing is clear: the rate of fossil-fuel extraction to meet demand growth is unsustainable. It's not a question of if but rather when fuel production begins to decline. You have a choice. You can stick your head in the sand and ignore peak oil or you can do something about it.

I believe in having two plans. Plan A is a plan for success, expecting that, as the pressures mount, there will be a new revolution in energy-efficiency technologies and clean-energy production, although the transition will be turbulent as oil prices rise sharply, leading to a zigzag in economic activity. This plan requires you to reorganise your balance sheet to take advantage of an extraordinary opportunity to grow your wealth and avoid being hit by high inflation, by ramping up investment in energy, commodities, energy efficiency, gold, index-linked bonds, etc. Nationally, it requires Ireland to step up the resources, incentives and speed at which it develops a green-energy, clean-technology economy. We should know within ten years if the world is succeeding in transitioning to a new energy age. If it doesn't we – all of us – will need a Plan B: a contingency, should our collective local and global efforts fail to bridge the yawning gap between energy production and energy demand.

Plan B is a fallback plan to move to a less complex world with much lower energy consumption levels. Nationally, Ireland needs to plan for extreme energy shortages, well beyond those envisaged by the Department of Communications, Energy and Natural Resources' 2008 plan to deal with temporary oil shortages. Central to such planning has to be the detail on how to get sufficient quantities of food to urban centres quickly, how to shift from mechanisation to labour-intensive agriculture, how to overhaul the country's education system to produce far more graduates with practical skills, and how to get private motorists to switch to public transport, especially to trains. Meanwhile, any investment you make now in self-sufficiency, energy efficiency and energy independence will help you a great deal in preparing for what will come quickly in your lifetime.

3. The Commodities Family

If you're anything like me, you too have become so used to the Age of Plenty that you've hardly ever paused to consider where everything comes from or, more importantly, if it can continue. Your gut tells you that there's a problem brewing but you don't know how to get its measure or assess its impact. You don't wake up in the morning dwelling on the fact that everything you'll do that day – from getting about, to eating and entertainment – is based on an abundant access to fossil fuels. Hasn't humankind reached a new level during our lifetimes when we can just about solve any problem with the marvels of technology, intensive food production and access to cheap labour markets in far-flung corners of the world to manufacture all our low-cost goods and services? Isn't that it? To get just about anything that your heart desires, all you have to do is go online or pop down to the local big box Woodies or Tesco and if your bank account can't stomach it, well, you can borrow it to pay back later.

In the Age of Plenty, we bought patio heaters that run on gas to keep ourselves warm outside so we can smoke in peace; we put monster engines on the back of powerboats that tear through delicate marine landscapes guzzling petrol as they bash through the waves; we were fixated with TV shows like *Top Gear* where big engines are pitted against each other to find the fastest, the strongest, the most desirable; and we demanded cheap seats on flights to just about anywhere, complaining about the lack of tea vouchers when things went wrong. Energy has been so cheap for thirty years that we've grown used to treating it like an abundant commodity, a cheap right that seems to just materialise in whatever quantity we demand and is paid for by our taxes and income. When electricity and gas prices rise, we bellow at the government and complain about the inefficiencies of our energy monopolies, without ever considering that maybe something more fundamental is afoot, like the opening of a new age characterised by scarcity pricing.

Whatever product or service you look at, its pricing is based on fossil fuels. Infrastructure and construction are reliant on metals mined all over the world, from Canada to Australia, but those metals not only need to be mined, they need to be processed and transported by ships and trucks to sites. Food is harvested worldwide on an industrial scale by machinery that is run on oil and it is boosted by phosphates and fertilisers that, in turn, depend on fossil fuels for their manufacture. Even the wonder of the age, the internet, is dependent on the manufacture of ever more powerful chips and PCs that are built in factories fed with fossil-fuel-based energy while the electricity that drives worldwide communication is powered, for the most part, from the same source. Everything is built on the platform of oil, gas and coal. Nuclear power plants are constructed and maintained using oil-based energy; wind turbines are reliant on steel; solar panels need other metals and are manufactured in plants dependent on fossil-fuel electricity.

The fact is that the modern world is constructed on a limited sea of oil, gas and coal from which it takes an irreversible and non-renewable drawdown every day. Oil is the base commodity and its price dictates to just about every other price – from metals to food, as energy input costs determine the price of mining and agriculture.

Yet the last time you may have read about commodities was probably in geography class when you were also struggling with *The Lord of the Rings*, pimples and your first love. Since then, it's been pretty much background noise, not surprising given that, during the Age of Plenty that began in the 1970s, commodities have been relatively cheap and the commodity market has lagged every other sector as an unsexy investment area. But that's changing as we enter the Age of Scarcity, so come on board a whistle-stop tour of commodities – the basic raw materials of the planet.

Three billion new consumers

Globalisation, free-trade agreements and the collapse of communist economics has added more than 3 billion new and modernised consumers to the global marketplace over the past twenty years. Vast and fast-growing economies, such as the BRIC (Brazil, Russia, India and China) group, plus a myriad others stretching across Asia to the Middle East, have created a sharply rising demand for the planet's natural resources. When these are in limited supply, whether due to depletion or underinvestment in the infrastructure needed to meet demand growth, prices rise. There is also artificial acceleration in prices because of investment speculation. The most essential ingredient in industrialisation is energy, which principally comes from oil, gas and coal. Rising energy costs are having an impact right across the global economy, as well as in other commodity markets, driving up the input costs involved in both producing goods and transporting them to consumers.

Oil driving population growth

Since the Second World War, the human population has nearly trebled and it continues to grow. Currently nearing 6.8 billion people, it is expected to expand to 9 billion by 2050. Starting in the nineteenth century, it took 130 years to add 1 billion people to the human population; now it takes just thirteen years. The rate at which the population has grown is directly correlated to oil production. The world is also urbanising at an accelerated rate. Just before the First World War, one in every seven of the world's population lived in urban areas. Today, it's one in two. By 2030 it is estimated that 60% of the global population will live in cities and towns. The expansion of the global metropolitan stock has placed a far greater demand on the natural resources needed for the construction industry.

In 1900, when the global population stood at about 1 billion people, oil output was about 1 mbpd. By the time the population doubled to 2 billion at the outbreak of the Second World War, oil consumption had reached 10 mbpd. By 2008, with the world population now reaching 6.5 billion and urbanising rapidly, oil consumption has touched 87 mbpd. At current rates of growth, oil consumption is expected by some to reach 120 mbpd by 2030. Global demand for natural gas and electricity is expected to jump 50% from current levels over the same period.

The growth in population means more manufacturing, food, transport, etc. – but just about more of everything else begins with the most basic input – energy. The world population could not have reached present-day levels, and cannot be expected to grow further, without mass commercialisation of energy sources such as oil, gas and coal. Logic tells us that the world population will plateau as natural resources become more limited. Just as logic tells us that, shorn of access to cheap fossil fuels, the population today would probably still be close to the same level as it was in 1900.

Energise

Oil

Oil is the king of commodities and accounts for 40% of global energy demand. The last energy crisis was triggered by the OPEC embargo on oil shipments to the US, triggering a 400% rise in its price, lengthy queues outside petrol stations and recessions. It also led to high double-digit inflation that lasted many years, increased unemployment and dealt a severe shock to the global economy.

Table 3.1 tells the tale. The figures for 2007 show that while the United States produced 8.46 mbpd and had reserves of 21 billion barrels, it consumed nearly three times more oil than it produced at 20.68 mbpd. Saudi Arabia, on the other hand, which produced 10.24 mbpd from reserves of 262 billion, barely makes it into the top ten consumers of oil. Russia is a major player, producing 9.87 mbpd with proven reserves of 60 billion but, with growing consumer demand within its own borders of 2.82 mbpd, its appetite for oil is growing and eating into its exports.

Controversy remains over the reserve estimates of Middle Eastern countries, with allegations that OPEC countries such as Saudi Arabia have reported 'paper barrels'. If proved, the allegations that reserves have been exaggerated to improve power within OPEC would substantially change the figures for proven reserves given in Table 3.1, and would worsen the problem of depletion further. A more recent examination of the world oil endowment has been undertaken by the IEA and is discussed in Chapter 5. The reserve estimates for Canada include its oil sands but, as noted earlier, extracting oil from sand is very different from and more costly than pumping it out of the ground.

OPEC represents a large chunk of oil producers and presently comprises twelve member countries: Algeria, Angola, Ecuador,

Table 3.1 The top oil players, 2007

	Producers		Reserves		Exporters		Consumers	
	Million barrels/day	Rank	Billion barrels	Rank	Million barrels/day	Rank	Million barrels/day	Rank
Saudi Arabia	10.243	1	262.3	1	8.038	1	2.210	10
Russia	9.874	2	60.0	8	7.054	2	2.820	4
USA	8.457	3	21.0	6	Not in top 15		20.680	1
Iran	4.034	4	136.3	3	2.326	5	1.708	14
China	3.912	5	16.0	13	Not in top 15		7.565	2
Mexico	3.500	6	12.4	15	1.381	13	2.119	11
Canada	3.400	7	179.2	2	1.058	15	2.364	8
UAE	2.948	8	97.8	6	Not in top 15		Not in top 15	
Venezuela	2.670	9	80.0	7	1.960	8	Not in top 15	
Kuwait	2.616	10	101.5	5	2.291	6	Not in top 15	
Norway	2.600	11	Not in top 15		2.340	4	Not in top 15	
Nigeria	2.400	12	36.2	10	2.082	7	Not in top 15	
Brazil	2.300	13	Not in top 15		Not in top 15		2.700	6
Algeria	2.200	14	Not in top 15		1.907	9	Not in top 15	

Table 3.1 (*continued*)

	Producers		Reserves		Exporters		Consumers	
	Million barrels/day	Rank	Billion barrels	Rank	Million barrels/day	Rank	Million barrels/day	Rank
Iraq	2.100	15	115.0	4	1.501	12	Not in top 15	
Libya	Not in top 15		41.5	9	1.584	11	Not in top 15	
Japan	Not in top 15		Not in top 15		Not in top 15		5.007	3
India	Not in top 15		Not in top 15		Not in top 15		2.800	5
Germany	Not in top 15		Not in top 15		Not in top 15		2.456	7
South Korea	Not in top 15		Not in top 15		Not in top 15		2.214	9
France	Not in top 15		Not in top 15		Not in top 15		1.950	12

Source: Based on 2007 data compiled by the US Energy Information Administration (EIA).

Note: Ireland is ranked 57th for consumption and 82nd for oil reserves; the UK is ranked 18th for oil production, 13th for oil consumption and 26th for oil reserves.

Iran, Iraq, Kuwait, Libya, Nigeria, Qatar, Saudi Arabia, the United Arab Emirates and Venezuela. Producing about 40% of the world oil supply, OPEC members hold about two-thirds of world reserves, but with output restrictions on other producers OPEC's power over the global market is growing. OPEC imposes quotas on its members to control the price of oil and, with Saudi Arabia as the world's largest producer, OPEC has been able to exercise swing power in the market, opening its taps more to pump oil at times of shortage.

Oil isn't of uniform quality or worth and comes in two main types: light and sweet, and heavy and sour. The yield or density of light and sweet crude oil is higher than the heavy and sour variety and it produces more refined products. The lower the sulphur content in crude oil, the better the quality, hence sweet crude is more valuable than sour crude. The typical yield from the average global barrel of refined oil is roughly half gasoline, a quarter diesel fuels and heating oil, a tenth jet fuel and the rest is made up of liquid petroleum gas, heavy fuel oil and other products.

Oil prices have been rising steadily since 1999 and, following a small dip between 2001 and 2002, the trend has been continuously upwards. As recently as 1998 oil prices were at less than $15 a barrel, peaking in 2000 at over $30 but dropping back in 2001 at just over $20. Since mid-2003, however, oil prices have been rising steadily. Many believed they had peaked when they hit $75 in 2006, but by mid-2008 oil was selling at close to $150 a barrel: ten times the price it had been ten years earlier.

Natural gas

Natural gas is responsible for meeting 25% of world energy demand. Like oil, it is a fossil fuel that has been created over millions of years by decayed matter under the surface of the earth. Natural gas comes from the same source as oil and the two often occur together. The largest users of natural gas are not consumers, but industry, which uses it for electrical generation and transport. Natural gas is not measured in gallons but in cubic metres and is principally made up of methane, which is a hydrocarbon molecule. Natural gas also contains other important hydrocarbons, such as propane, ethane and butane, all of which have industrial applications and are used in everything from food processing and metal smelting to waste incineration and firing industrial boilers.

Table 3.2 Top fifteen natural gas proven reserves, 2009

Country	Rank	Reserves (trillion m³)
Russia	1	43.300
Iran	2	28.080
Qatar	3	25.260
Saudi Arabia	4	7.319
United States	5	6.731
UAE	6	6.071
Nigeria	7	5.215
Venezuela	8	4.840
Algeria	9	4.502
Iraq	10	3.170
Indonesia	11	3.001
Turkmenistan	12	2.662
China	13	2.460
Kazakhstan	14	2.407
Malaysia	15	2.350

Source: CIA World Factbook, estimates for start of 2009. Ireland is ranked 79th; the UK is ranked 37th.

But natural gas is also used in many countries for home heating and cooking. It's heavily used to generate electricity and its strongest growing sector is liquefied natural gas, created by super-cooling and compressing natural gas into a transportable liquid.

Natural gas is subject to the same demand pressure as oil. In 2005 the total amount of natural gas needed to meet worldwide demand was approximately 100 trillion cubic feet, but with a rate of growth estimated at 2.3% a year, annual demand will double to over 200 trillion cubic feet by 2040.

Russia is the major player in the natural gas marketplace, occupying the top position among producers of natural gas worldwide, and it is essential to European supply – a fact that was brought into harsh relief when the Putin administration cut off supplies to the Ukraine and disrupted European markets.

Coal

Coal, which had been the dominant fuel in manufacturing since the advent of the industrial age in the mid-1700s, was replaced by oil as the principal source of energy worldwide as recently as the early 1900s. Today, coal is primarily used for electricity generation and steel manufacturing. Coal is regarded as an abundant solid fossil fuel, but finding new, high-quality coal deposits is becoming harder. Its combustion also produces the highest carbon emissions. Coal is also largely consumed by the countries in which it is produced. The United States has the largest reserves of coal in the world at over 246,600 million short tons in 2005. Russia has the second largest reserves at 157,000 million short tons with China coming in third at 114,500 million short tons.

Much like oil, coal comes in varying qualities. The best quality is anthracite, which gives the highest energy output, while lignite gives the least amount of energy and has the highest sulphur content. The two other types of coal are sub-bituminous, which is a slightly better quality than lignite and which is principally used for electricity generation, and bituminous, which is the most common coal used for home heating and electricity generation.

Driven by rising demand for ever more energy to meet its rapidly growing economy, China is the largest exploiter of its coal reserves in the world, processing nearly twice as much coal as the United States at just under 1,000 million short tons in 2005.

Soft commodities

Coffee

Unlike energy and metals, soft commodities are both seasonal and edible! Coffee is the second most traded commodity in the world after oil and its production is dominated by, in rank order, Brazil, Colombia, Vietnam, Indonesia and India. There are two main bean types and, as with most commodities, there are differences in quality. The Arabica bean, responsible for 60% of global production, is the top coffee bean and commands the highest price. Less expensive than Arabica, Robusta beans account for the remaining 40% of global coffee production.

Coffee features heavily in mixed commodity funds because of its sheer scale, but if you want to focus on it, one way of doing so is to invest in coffee retailers like **Starbucks (NASDAQ: SBUX)** or choose an ETC that focuses on coffee. Starbucks is a giant in the coffee market, with more than 10,000 shops worldwide and operating in thirty countries; in mid-2009 it had a market capitalisation of about $10 billion and was trading at a little over $13 a share. Keep in mind the risk associated with being overly reliant on any one company's shares. Ask yourself, what is the likely impact on exotic coffee shops as the cost of long-distance shipping rises with oil prices in the future? Who drinks exotic coffees and how far are they from where the coffee is grown? What oil premium will Starbucks customers pay to continue to sip their favourite drink?

Cocoa

Grown principally in equatorial regions, cocoa is the dried and fermented seed of the cacao tree and it is the main ingredient used in making chocolate. The largest cocoa producer in the world is the Ivory Coast, followed by Ghana, Indonesia, Nigeria and Brazil.

Sugar

Sugar has been used as a food stuff for millennia. It is a major ingredient in processed foods and in sweeteners. The top producer in the world is Brazil, producing over 27 million tons of sugar in 2005, followed by India at 26 million tons and China at 15 million tons. Total worldwide sugar production is in excess of 200 million tons per year.

Corn

Worldwide corn production is in excess of 700 million metric tons per year and, much like other commodities, comes in several grades. The United States dominates the world corn market, producing about a third of world supply. China is the second largest producer at about a sixth of world supply.

Wheat

Wheat was originally measured in bushels (each bushel accounted for 60lb of wheat) and it is the world's oldest traded commodity. Worldwide, wheat production is in excess of 600 million metric tons a year with China, India and the US dominating the top three positions. Other major producers include France, Russia, Canada and Australia.

Soya beans

Soya beans are used for the creation of vegetable oil and as a feed-stock. The oil is used for cooking and for the manufacture of bio-diesel. Soya bean meal is a by-product of soya bean oil manufacture and is used as a high-energy food for poultry and cattle.

The United States is the largest producer of soya beans in the world accounting for more than 50% of the market, with Brazil second, accounting for 20%.

Metals

Consider how much metal goes into building new cities like Shanghai or into renewing and expanding the world's 700 million vehicles and you'll quickly realise just what a big business metal mining has become. Metals can be split into two broad categories: precious metals and base metals. Precious metals are used largely in jewellery making and as a store of value, whereas base metals are used in industrial processes.

Precious metals

GOLD

Gold is the benchmark precious metal. Not only is gold a store of value, especially at a time of rising inflation and declining currency strength (particularly the dollar), but it is also a commodity in its own right and is used in jewellery manufacture and in certain industrial processes. Towards the end of the Second World War, in an accord known as the Bretton Woods Agreement, forty-four of the world's wealthiest countries, including the US, pegged their currencies to gold. In 1971 President Richard Nixon removed the dollar from the gold standard so the world's reserve currency is no longer backed by gold.

The last gold bull market coincided with the heavy inflationary period of the 1970s, when gold prices grew by 33.7% per annum. Gold does badly at times of stable economic growth when investment in financial assets is in vogue, but springs to life as soon as inflation threatens. Until the early 1970s, gold was at a fixed price of $35 a troy ounce and started to trade freely in 1975 at $200 a troy ounce, reaching an all-time high of $850 on 21 January 1980. A troy ounce is the equivalent to 31.1g of gold. After languishing unloved throughout most of the 1980s and all of the 1990s, gold has, in recent years, started into another bull market and by mid-2008 was trading at over $900 per troy ounce. Gold is measured in metric tons by central banks with each ton containing 32,150 troy ounces. Gold's quality or purity is measured by carats, with 24 carats representing 100% purity.

There are several ways in which you can invest in gold. Using specialists, such as Dublin-based GoldCore, you can order gold coins, for example: Krugerrands from South Africa, Eagles from

Table 3.3 Top ten gold reserves

Reserves	Rank	Metric tons
USA	1	8,133.5
Germany	2	3,412.6
International Monetary Fund	3	3,217.3
France	4	2,452.8
Italy	5	2,451.8
China	6	1,054.0
Switzerland	7	1,040.1
Japan	8	765.3
Netherlands	9	612.5
European Central Bank	10	536.0

Source: Based on World Gold Council statistics for the first quarter of 2009.

Note: Ireland is ranked 74th with 5.5 metric tons.

Table 3.4 Gold purity

Carats	Purity
24k	100.00%
22k	91.67%
18k	75.00%
14k	58.33%
10k	41.67%
9k	37.50%

the United States, Pandas from China and Sovereigns from the United Kingdom. Gold coins come in various measures from 1/10th of an ounce to 1 ounce and usually at 22 carats in quality. Another way to invest in gold is to buy Perth Mint Certificates from an authorised Perth Mint agency such as GoldCore. Typically, there is an entry cost of 3%, but your gold doesn't move and stays in the Perth Mint in Australia. The market is highly liquid and, unlike physical storage at home, there are no security risks.

For those who prefer trading, a better way to invest in gold is through an exchange-traded fund such as ETF Securities' **Gold Bullion Securities (London: GBS)**. There are no entry costs and the fund management charge is 0.4% a year. Bear in mind that you don't hold the gold, instead it is held by counter parties, which adds an additional layer of risk. Investing in exchange-traded funds can be undertaken from any tax jurisdiction through a local or international stockbroker, but you should first check on the tax treatment on gains. The domestic life-assurance industry will be quick to get in on the game by investing in exchange-traded funds, but by adding an extra layer of costs to do so. For example in Ireland in July 2009 Zurich Life, previously known as Eagle Star Life, issued a unit-linked fund that invests in the Gold Bullion Securities ETF. Although these unit-linked funds will come at higher costs, you have the flexibility to switch into other funds within the Zurich Life fund range without triggering a capital gains tax liability. If you are an Irish taxpayer, no tax is payable for a period of eight years, at which point you are required to pay 28% tax on any profits made to the Revenue Commissioners.

You can get a leveraged (or geared) rate of return on gold by investing in a leveraged gold-bullion ETF or by investing in gold-mining companies either through stock picking or through a gold-mining ETF. However, this is very different from investing directly in the commodity itself, since mining may be affected by other influences such as natural disasters, political considerations and war or civil unrest. The two largest gold-mining companies in the world are Barrick Gold and Newmont Mining (see page 77). In the event of a long-run commodity bull market, the scope for increases in gold prices and other precious metals is high.

Throughout the 1990s, gold went through a prolonged bear market spell reaching a low of close to $250 per troy ounce in 1999. The big comeback in gold coincided with rising oil prices and the decline in the dollar, which was largely triggered by the scale of US debt.

SILVER

Silver is used both for jewellery and in industrial processes such as welding, electrical conduction and photography. The top silver producer in the world is Peru, which produced over 100 million ounces of silver in 2006, followed closely by Mexico at over 90 million ounces and Australia at over 77 million ounces. You can buy silver coins or you can invest in exchange-traded funds that track the spot market for silver. At the close of 2009 silver was trading at very low prices relative to gold, which surged past $1,100 per ounce while silver languished at $18 – a more than sixtyfold differential. The long-term relationship between gold and silver is sixteenfold not sixtyfold, suggesting that, relative to gold, silver has some catching up to do.

PLATINUM

Platinum is the rarest of precious metals and is the name given to a group of metals that also includes palladium, iridium, rhodium, ruthenium and osmium. South Africa is the largest platinum producer and accounts for 90% of global reserves. Much like gold and silver, platinum has also been enjoying a strong run as a store of value, i.e. a safe haven in times of rising inflation and a declining dollar. Platinum is also used in the manufacture of catalytic converters, which accounts for nearly 50% of global platinum demand.

Platinum enjoys high conductivity characteristics for electricity and is widely used across industry from fibreoptic cables to microchips.

Base metals

Demand for base metals such as steel, aluminium and copper has been moving sharply upwards in line with industrialisation and infrastructure booms in China, India, Russia and Brazil. In 1950 there were just nine urban areas in the world with populations in excess of 5 million. The projected number of urban populations in excess of 5 million by 2015 is estimated at fifty-three, with over half of these being in Asia. Base metals are vital ingredients to meet the construction demand due to this trend towards urbanisation.

STEEL

Steel, which is a by-product of iron, is the metal most traded. The top ten steel-producing countries account for three-quarters of global steel production, with China dominating at over 30%. In 2009 China produced in excess of 567 million metric tons. Japan is the world's second largest producer followed by the US, Russia and South Korea.

The largest European-based steel producer is **ArcelorMittal SA (NYSE: MT)** with a market capitalisation of $39 billion in mid-2009. It was formed by a recent merger, designed to create economies of scale to control in excess of 10% of the world's production. ArcelorMittal has steel operations in twenty countries and produces 35% of its steel in the Americas, 46% in Europe and 19% in other countries such as South Africa, Kazakhstan, Algeria and Morocco. Just as in any other sector, there is an ETF that will spread your investment across steel companies throughout the world such as the **Russell Global Steel Large Cap Index (London: STEE)**, available from ETF Securities.

ALUMINIUM

Aluminium's resistance to corrosion and its lightness accounts for its wide use in everything from transport to soft drinks cans. Much like many of the other metals, the price of aluminium has been rising steadily since 2003. One way of gaining a play on aluminium exposed to the fast-growing Chinese economy is to invest in the Beijing-based **Aluminium Corporation of China (NYSE: ACH)**. The company specialises in producing aluminium from its bauxite mines for both the Chinese and international markets.

COPPER

Copper is widely used throughout the world in electricity conductors, in engineering and in industrial processes. When alloyed with tin, it produces bronze; when alloyed with zinc, it produces brass; and when alloyed with nickel, it produces cupronickel, an important alloy in marine engineering that is also used to manufacture coins, including the US nickel. **Freeport-McMoRan Copper & Gold Inc. (NYSE: FCX)**, with a market capitalisation mid-2009 of $20 billion, has mining operations in countries with significant copper ore, such as Indonesia and Papua New Guinea, and also mines gold and molybdenum, a mineral whose name comes from the Greek for 'lead-like' that is used in making high-strength steel alloys.

4. Investing in Commodities

You don't have to trade in futures or expect to become expert in the complicated world of commodity behaviour, where you need to anticipate rises and falls in prices with Merlin-like accuracy. All you need is a little common sense and a belief that conventional investment funds and thinking hasn't yet cottoned on to the dawning of the Age of Scarcity. When you've committed (and ideally not at the top of a pro-cycle speculative bubble), the length of time you stay in markets should do the rest for you, even if the ride is bumpy.

The argument to diversify into commodities for at least the next ten to twenty years is compelling, but how much should you commit? This is the killer question. Conventional portfolio thinking limits investment in energy to no more than 10%, evident from the asset mix that comprises the common-or-garden variety balanced funds that dominate Irish retail investment space. This is substantial underexposure, given the forces now unleashed. We have entered an unprecedented economic cycle, one characterised by rising energy and food inflation to which many conventional investment tactics are negatively exposed. That means they'll shed truckloads of money. How much you can shift from your current balance-sheet mix is a question only you can truly answer, but the typical Irish balance sheet is already heavily skewed towards Irish property, which accounts for about two-thirds of most Irish wealth.

You don't have to be reminded that Irish property is illiquid, slow and expensive to offload and divestment can trigger a capital gains tax liability but, faced with the likelihood of a pretty damp future for capital growth, the switching costs become less unattractive if the new asset class is raring to go higher. Remember, it is not the number of eggs you have in the basket, but the behaviour of the eggs against one another, that's the key. It is for this reason that it makes a lot of sense to have an uncorrelated mix of diversified assets, particularly one that is biased towards commodities and energy. But don't expect leadership from conventional investment advisors, like stockbrokers, who've tied up most of their clients' money in assets that won't perform well in the Age of Scarcity and are wedded to investment models that predate the most recent energy crisis. For many of them, peak oil is as alien as the lunar landscape.

In 2006, the Irish National Pension Reserve Fund had approximately two-thirds of its holdings in general equities, 13% in bonds, 8% in property and just 2% in commodities. The remainder was in private equity, cash and alternative assets. In a study undertaken by *You & Your Money* magazine in June 2008, Irish pension funds were found to be little different with an average energy exposure of just 8%. So how do you invest in commodities reasonably safely?

Investing in individual commodities is a tricky business and not for the fainthearted or inexperienced. Commodities are traded in the futures market. One of the best ways to understand the futures market is to consider airlines like Ryanair and Aer Lingus who buy oil futures to hedge their position against rising jet fuel prices. They enter into an agreement to buy a fixed amount of fuel at a fixed price for a fixed period of time. The futures markets are used not just by commercial players, such as airlines, but also by traders, investors and speculators. The major exchanges for commodities futures include the New York Mercantile Exchange (NYMEX) and the Chicago Mercantile Exchange (CME). You can invest directly in commodities futures, but don't go near them unless you've first studied commodity trading, the skills for which are beyond the scope of this book. Neither should you over-concentrate on any single commodity nor any single mining stock, although mega-miners, like BHP Billiton (discussed later), represent partial diversification in commodity mining. One of the most practical ways to avoid over-concentration on any one particular commodity or stock is to delegate the task to professional fund managers.

It's a fund world!

Whatever investment strategy you wish to follow, check out the new world of exchange-traded commodities and funds from innovative players like ETF Securities. Here you'll find a range of ETCs that cover just about every energy, metal and food commodity traded, with options to use leverage if you have the appetite. You'll also find exchange-traded funds that invest across a range of stocks in companies that operate in the commodity markets. But be warned: familiarise yourself with the details that will help you understand the riskiness of each fund, its charges, its security and its regulation. Leveraged funds use financing to provide additional exposure, usually twice the exposure, to the underlying commodity, be it gold, petroleum, corn or whatever. This increases the potential return but doubles the risk of losses. Unlike borrowing personally to invest, however, the method of leveraging used is non-recourse – in other words, the debt is ring-fenced within the fund. You can only lose what you've invested.

If you find ETCs and ETFs as daunting as picking stocks, you could simply rely upon brands with which you're familiar, household names with funds in the game.

One of my favourite stock-picking commodity funds is **JPMorgan's Global Natural Resources Fund**. This is an actively managed fund, where the investment managers pick and choose what to hold and when, on your behalf, as distinct from passive funds that go on auto-pilot by tracking indices. JPMorgan is one of the largest asset managers in the world and has been in the business of managing investment in commodities since the mid-1960s. Its Global Natural Resources Fund is available under an open-ended investment company registered at the Luxembourg Financial Services Centre and administered through London. In 2009, the fund had nearly €2 billion invested across a range of global commodity companies, including well-known firms such as BHP Billiton (base metal and diversified), Petrobras (energy), and Kinross Gold (gold and precious metals). For example, at the end of the first quarter 2009, the weighting of the fund was: 29.1% energy; 35.8% gold and precious metals; 26.1% base metals and diversified; 2.4% diamonds and other; 2.4% soft commodities and 3.8% in cash and was diversified across Canada, 32%; Australia, 17%; United Kingdom, 21%; and United States, 7% with the remainder spread elsewhere.

The fund manager decides the allocation across commodities and when to buy and sell stocks, but, since it's a fund and not a direct investment in stocks, there is no capital gains tax levied on profit taking or income tax on dividends. Qualifying in Ireland as an Undertaking for Collective Investment in Transferable Securities (UCITS), there is full transparency on all charges and audited accounts. The total annual management charge is 1.5%; however, in addition, there are extra expenses accounting for 0.4% a year. The initial entry cost of 5% can be reduced to as low as 0.25% by negotiating commission discounts with qualifying intermediaries simply by stating at the outset that you want a cut in their commission before you do business. There are redemption costs of 0.5%.

Less sophisticated routes into the commodities markets can be undertaken through passive unit-linked funds administered by Irish life-assurance companies that track indices. These are packaged as unit-linked single-premium life policies. The charges usually displayed are those of the life office. You do not get audited accounts and the total expenses of the fund are not published. These funds invest in commodity indices but, remember, you can access these indices directly and bypass the life offices acting as middlemen. Nevertheless, for many investors, unit-linked funds are attractive, convenient and available from trusted, local and well-known brands despite adding an additional layer of costs. Unit-linked funds perform an important role by bringing the commodity story to investors on the ground through life offices' direct and intermediary networks. They also provide the opportunity to diversify across a series of funds within the fund family without triggering capital gains tax, an advantage over direct investment in markets.

Although embryonic, there are a number of fund choices now available in the Irish market. Zurich Life administers the **Earth Resources Fund**. This is a nicely balanced unit-linked fund that invests in a range of indices across oil, alternative energy, precious metals and soft commodities. The **ETFS Brent Oil** invests 100% in oil while the **Powershares Wilderhill Clean Energy Portfolio** is spread across renewable energy, 36%; power delivery and conservation, 24%; energy storage, 13%; cleaner fuels, 12%; energy conversion, 10%; and greener utilities, 5%. At the end of 2007, the **ETFS Physical Precious Metals Basket** was gold, 42%; silver, 26%; platinum, 20%; and palladium, 12%. The **ETFS Agriculture DY-AIGCI** spreads across the major soft commodities: soya bean oil, 10%; coffee, 10%; sugar, 11%; cotton, 8%; wheat, 16%; corn, 19%; and soya beans, 26%.

Irish Life also offers a **Commodity Index Fund** that invests exclusively in indices managed by Goldman Sachs, i.e. 50% into the Goldman Sachs Commodity Total Return Index (GSCI) and 50% in Goldman Sachs Non-Energy Total Return Index (GSNE). By mid-2008 the asset mix was: energy, 39%; industrial metals, 17%; precious metals, 5%; livestock, 9%; and agriculture, 30%.

One of the most interesting Irish funds is administered by New Ireland, but managed by KBC Asset Management Limited. **The KBCAM Eco Alternative Energy Fund** does not invest in indices, but rather invests directly in PLCs and is actively managed. By the end of the first quarter of 2008, its holdings included names familiar in alternative energy, many of which you'll find in later chapters, such as Vestas Wind Systems (Denmark), Gamesa (Spain), Iberdrola Renovables (Spain), Fortum (Finland) and First Solar Inc. (USA). This fund provides a diversified play across the alternative energy spectrum, including wind, utilities, solar, fuel cells and biomass. Reflecting the European lead in green energy directives, the geographical spread of the fund is Euroland 49%; North America, 25%; rest of Europe, 18%; and rest of the world, 8%.

Water, water everywhere

Worldwide sales by the water industry of fresh water, or blue gold as it is sometimes called, trail those of oil and electricity by a long way but, with demand growth exceeding supply growth just as in the oil market, the same tension is pushing up prices.

Fresh water from global precipitation averages 110 cubic kilometres each year, but a little over 10% restocks the underground aquifers, lakes and rivers upon which we depend. Population growth at 80 million annually and rising standards of living are increasing the strain on fresh-water supplies, which are especially under pressure because of demand from agriculture to grow crops to meet sharply rising food demand. The UN estimates that by 2030 the world population will be using up to 90% of global fresh-water supply, in comparison with a level of about 54% today. Already, a sixth of the world population doesn't have access to fresh water and another third are struggling with shortages. In the developed world, water levels are at an all-time low in many great rivers, lakes and river deltas. Aquifers are depleting in India, China, large parts of Asia and in the former Soviet bloc, and water shortages are becoming a regular feature across many parts of Europe as far north as the UK.

Consider the link between oil and water in key oil producers like Saudi Arabia and other Middle Eastern countries whose economies and populations are growing quickly. Saudi Arabia may have oil reserves that dwarf domestic oil demand but it has precious little water, having depleted its underground water reserves by half over the past fifteen years. The answer to its food security, which is dependent on water, is sea-water desalination, a process that burns up vast quantities of energy. As a region, the Middle East is expected to take 1 million barrels of oil off world markets over the next fifteen years as the feedstock for the desalination of water for domestic and agricultural consumption.

Offering an even split between water technologies and utilities globally is the **ETFS Janney Global Water Fund** (WATE), an ETF quoted in London that was launched as recently as November 2008. Alternatively, you could go for a seasoned active manager in this sector – the **KBCAM Eco Water Fund**, available through the New Ireland fund family. This is an actively managed fund concentrating on companies that produce, manufacture and provide equipment in the water sector. In the first quarter of 2009, the fund was 26% invested in water technologies, 37% in water and waste water and 37% in water infrastructure with a range of holdings. The largest concentration of the fund is in North America, 44%; followed by Euroland 18%; rest of Europe, 17%; and the rest of the world, 21%.

Unit-linked funds are issued as single-premium, whole-of-life policies by domestic Irish life offices. These products are not as transparent as other types of collective investments, such as open-ended investment companies or where you buy ETFs directly on stock exchanges. In Ireland, backend-loaded pricing structures have become common. This means that although 100% of our monies are invested from day one, there are backend charges should you cash in early – typically, within the first five years. These early exit charges usually commence at 5% in year one and decline to 0% after five years. They are used to recover sales and marketing expenses, including the payment of commission to intermediaries. By negotiating on commission, you will be in a position to increase the investment allocation from 100% to as high as 104%, offsetting the early exit charges almost entirely.

Annual fund management charges are typically between 1.25% and 1.75%, but bear in mind that these may not fully reflect the true look-through charges, such as stockbroker fees, etc., in the background. It is more likely that when all fund operating costs are taken into account total annual expenses run closer to 2% a year. Fund prices are lower in larger markets that enjoy higher competitive forces and larger economies of scale but the advent of funds that are quoted on stock markets, rather than distributed through traditional channels, such as life offices and banks, has opened up the opportunity to all investors to invest in funds cheaply, wherever you may be located.

Investing in CRAB!

Four countries are consistently cited as locations rich in energy sources, minerals and metals. Collectively, they are known as CRAB – Canada, Russia, Australia and Brazil – and all four stand to gain strongly as net exporters. The scramble for depleting natural resources will heat their stock markets and surplus exports over imports will strengthen their currencies relative to resource-poor countries and regions. Even the populous behemoths of China and India do not enjoy long-term competitive advantage since their main resource, cheaper labour, will erode as inflation eats into their economic growth. This is already happening.

Examine the top stocks in CRAB captured by ETFs and you'll quickly find how much each stock market is juicy in materials and energy. Table 4.1 tells the tale.

GDP per capita in Canada (€16,700) and Australia (€15,000), both mature economies with lower domestic demand growth for their own natural resources, is much higher than for Russia (€1,700) and Brazil (€2,600), who are both playing catch-up. Tiger economic growth in Russia and in Brazil means that these countries will eat

Table 4.1 Stocks in Canada, Russia, Australia and Brazil captured by ETF

Country	Canada	Russia	Australia	Brazil
ETF Symbol	EWC	RSX	EWA	EWZ
Energy in ETF	24%	43%	9%	24%
Materials in ETF	12%	25%	28%	33%

EWC: iShares MSCI Canada Index Fund on AMEX; RSX: Market Vector Russia ETF on AMEX; EWA: iShares MSCI Australia Index Fund on AMEX; EWZ: iShares Inc. MSCI Brazil Free Index Fund on AMEX.

into their own natural resources first and export second. Russia comes with a relatively higher political risk, so you should probably weight any spread in CRAB a little more towards Canada and Australia and a little less towards Russia and Brazil.

The great advantage of ETFs is that they are traded daily and are liquid. Charges are also cheaper than actively managed funds and unit-linked funds, some of which simply provide wrappers around ETFs. But higher returns and a better understanding of commodities result from reasoned investment in a concentrated basket of shares. It makes perfect sense to do both: to invest in funds, actively managed and index tracking; but also to invest in selected shares, especially a portfolio of stocks that includes smaller companies that have not yet grown in size to become the type of stocks that larger funds buy (see later).

Risks

The techniques needed in day trading stocks or commodity indices are beyond the scope of this book, which instead encourages a buy-and-hold long-term strategy. This means investing in good funds and good companies that you have researched and it means being prepared to hold these through thick and thin. You can't make money without taking investment risk. That means taking on market risk, exposing your money to the sharp ups and downs of market conditions, because, even in a bull cycle, there will be speculative bubbles and bursts.

The world's natural resources aren't necessarily always available in its most stable regions. For example, the lion's share of oil is based in the Middle East, which is plagued with geopolitical risks exacerbated by the American-led invasion of Iraq and tensions between the West and Iran, which may be building nuclear weapons. The ugly irony of these tensions is that an outbreak of hostility would see oil prices shooting into the stratosphere along with those of just about every other energy stock outside of the Middle East. Natural resources are also plagued by political interference, market agreements and structures, like OPEC, designed to limit competition and maintain strong prices for its members.

International tensions about the control of and access to natural resources are ever present. In recent years Russia, for example, has been exercising political control over the Ukraine by cutting off its gas supplies and threatening Europe with the same. Russia also invaded South Ossetia, triggering a brief war with Georgia in 2008, across whose territory 1% of global oil production flows in a vital pipeline stretching from the Caspian Sea region to Turkey's coast. In 2006 Bolivia made the decision to nationalise its natural gas industry, wiping out positions held by international energy companies there. So don't underestimate the impact of politics on commodities.

Civilisations have fallen because of an inability to acquire sufficient quantities of energy, food and metals. Societies that have managed to control access to natural resources have survived and those that have failed have become extinct. The Spanish conquistadores' pillage of Peru and Mexico, destroying both the Aztec and Inca cultures, was driven by gold. The bloody Boer War, fought between the Dutch settlers and the British Empire, was over access to South Africa's minerals and metals. The Iraqi invasion of Kuwait, which led to the 1991 Persian Gulf War, was driven by oil, as, almost certainly, was the 2003 invasion of Iraq, led by the US, the world's largest single consumer of the stuff. The US military in Iraq uses eight times as much oil per day as its Second World War counterpart due to the increase in oil-fuelled equipment since the 1940s. The US military is the single biggest consumer of oil on the planet, using one of every 200 barrels produced worldwide. The Chinese military is growing at pace with its economy, as is Chinese demand for energy. Sino-US relations are likely to dominate most of this century. The key issue will be access to energy.

There may be bubbles ahead

The biggest market risk in commodities comes from speculation. Speculation is as old as time, of course, but today there is a new kind of speculation in commodity markets. In recent years, there has been a very substantial growth in investment by institutional investors, contributing significantly to food and energy price inflation. These investors include pension funds, sovereign wealth funds and other institutional investors who've decided to allocate a certain percentage of monies to commodities futures. These investors behave differently from commercial speculators, who add to the liquidity of the market. Their movement into commodities was driven by the equity bear market of 2000 to 2002 as investors eyed commodities, previously regarded with disdain, as a new asset class suitable for institutional investment.

The amount of money pouring into the commodities futures markets has grown from an estimated €13 billion at the end of 2003 to €260 billion by early 2008. Over the same period of time, prices of the twenty-five commodities that compose indices such as the Standard & Poor's-Goldman Sachs Commodities Index rose by an average of more than 180%.

In the oil market, the increased demand for oil from China grew over the same period by 920 million barrels of oil, an increase from 1.88 to 2.8 billion barrels, but speculation in petroleum futures increased by 848 million barrels, so the increase in demand from China had been matched by the increase in speculation by 2008. Speculation was not just limited to oil. Increased speculation was happening in other commodities such as US corn production, which is used both as food and as a raw material for ethanol. Institutional investors purchased more than 2 billion bushels of corn futures over the five years to 2008 and owned enough corn futures to stockpile the US demand for ethanol for an entire year. Speculators were already holding 1.3 billion bushels of wheat, enough to supply the US market with all the bread, pasta and baked goods it can eat for two years.

Unlike traditional speculators, who come to the market looking for value and who usually trade in and out quite quickly, institutional investors come with a different mindset. These investors have a predetermined allocation from a much larger fund invested in commodities futures, taking a buy-and-hold position almost regardless of current price, and their price insensitivity artificially swells current prices. Since commodities futures markets are much smaller than general equity markets, an increase in speculation volume has a greater impact on futures. World equity markets, valued at $44 trillion in 2004, are more than 240 times bigger than the twenty-five index commodities, so the relative impact of a modest redirection of cash from one into the other is very large.

A large increase in speculation creates a self-inflating bubble: as the increase in price attracts more speculators, prices increase further. Eventually the bubble bursts and prices return to their fundamental value – much like Irish property from 2007 forward. The new breed of index speculation amounts to a hoarding of commodities futures markets. Unlike commercial investors, these use the markets differently and will create speculative bubbles. So, while the underlying trend is sharply upwards due to population growth and global economic demand, expect plenty of bruising periods along the way as speculative bubbles grow and burst. The ideal timing, as ever, is to buy after there has been a major sell-off, before the market's underlying upward trend resumes.

Buying shares in commodity mining majors

One of the best ways to invest in commodities is to invest in large, diversified mining companies. The biggest on the block is **BHP Billiton (NYSE: BHP)**, valued by mid-2009 at $146 billion and formed by a giant merger in 2001 between Anglo-Dutch company Billiton and an Australian company Broken Hill Proprietary. BHP Billiton was involved in a failed €180 billion bid for rival mining group Rio Tinto, which was founded in 1872 by the Rothschild banking family. BHP Billiton is quoted on a number of stock exchanges, the nearest large stock exchange being London, but it's also quoted in New York. With headquarters in Melbourne, Australia, BHP Billiton has mining operations in more than twenty-five countries, including Canada, the US, South Africa and Australia. It is particularly strong in metal mining, especially aluminium, silver, copper and iron, but it also has investments in oil and natural gas.

Rio Tinto PLC (NYSE: RTP) is another major mining corporation. It has a market capitalisation of $55 billion and remains a takeover target for its bigger rival BHP Billiton. With headquarters in the UK, Rio Tinto involves itself in mining, in transportation and in the distribution of products, including aluminium, copper and gold, as well as industrial minerals such as borates, titanium dioxide, salt and talc, and iron ore. It also has interests in diamonds, producing nearly 30% of global natural diamonds, principally through its mining operations in Australia. Rio Tinto's mining activities are strongly represented in Australia and North America, but it also has significant operations in South America, Asia, Europe and South Africa.

Anglo–American PLC (NASDAQ : AAUK), with a market value in mid-2009 of $34 billion, produces 37% of global platinum supply from its mining operations in South Africa and gets a return from the highly restricted diamond market through its 45% ownership of De Beers with the balance held by Central Holdings Ltd, an Oppenheimer family company (40%), and the Government of Botswana (15%). Anglo-American also mines copper, nickel, zinc and iron ore.

Barrick Gold Corporation (NYSE: ABX), with headquarters in Toronto, was capitalised by the market in mid-2009 at $37 billion. Barrick has twenty-seven operating mines located in gold-rich districts in North America (35%), South America (32%), Africa (16%) and Australia Pacific (17%). In 2007, for the fifth year in a row, Barrick met its production estimates, producing more than 8 million ounces of gold at an average cost of $350 per troy ounce. Barrick also produced over 400 million pounds of copper. In 2008, Barrick was reckoned to have proven and probable gold reserves of 124.6 million ounces, making it the largest in the gold-mining industry. It also has 6.2 billion pounds of copper reserves and 1.03 billion ounces of silver.

Newmont Mining Corporation (NYSE: NEM), with a market capitalisation in mid-2009 at $23 billion, is a US-based gold-mining specialist, with headquarters in Colorado. It ranks as one of the largest gold-mining companies in the world with operations in the US (Nevada and California), Canada, Australia, Indonesia, Bolivia, Peru and Uzbekistan. Newmont has most recently moved into mining gold in Ghana, where it has over 20 million ounces of gold reserves. Founded in 1921, Newmont Mining Corporation employs or contracts about 34,000 people worldwide and also mines copper and silver. At the end of 2006, the company reported gold reserves of 93.9 million ounces. It has been following a merger-and-acquisitions strategy to improve efficiency by gaining larger scale. In May 1997 Newmont merged with Santa Fe Pacific Gold Corp. and in June 2000 it merged with Battle Mountain Gold Company. More recently, in 2002, Newmont acquired Normandy Mining Limited and Franco-Nevada Mining Corporation to become one of the world's gold-mining heavyweights.

For a wild card and more speculative investment in gold mining, **Jinshan Gold Mines Inc. (Toronto: JIN)** is interesting. With a market capitalisation of just $120 million, Jinshan is a minnow compared to the massive values of Barrick and Newmont; however, what makes it worth checking out is that Canadian company Ivanhoe Mines sold its 42% controlling stake in Jinshan to China National Gold Group, which, in turn, produces 20% of Chinese gold and accounts for 30% of China's known gold reserves with sixty-five gold mines. In five years, Jinshan has grown from a small exploration-stage mining company to one that holds one of China's largest gold-producing mines. Its continued growth will be based on merger-and-acquisition opportunities, financed by raising capital on the Hong Kong and Shanghai stock exchanges.

Fugro (London: FUGRceu) (Amsterdam: FUGRc), with a market capitalisation of €2.2 billion, specialises in high-tech support services for customers in the oil, gas and mining industries and construction in the search for natural resources. Fugro provides services in the collection and analysis of data relating to the earth's surface, sea bed, soils and rocks. Founded in 1962, Fugro has 12,000 employees in fifty countries and has a wide range of data-collection equipment including fifty aircraft and helicopters, more than a hundred remotely operated vehicles (ROVs), fifty vessels and four autonomous underwater vehicles (AUVs), as well as advanced satellite-positioning systems. Fugro is a world leader in pioneering technologies for remotely controlled agricultural operations using GPS technology.

Potash is a high-grade fertiliser and is the third most powerful crop nutrient after nitrogen and phosphate. (The word, derived from the Dutch word *potasch*, meaning wood ash, comes from the practice by early pioneers of extracting potassium fertiliser (K_2CO_3) by leaching wood ashes and evaporating the solution in large pots.) The price of potash is rising strongly and, by mid-2008, was heading for a record $1,000 a tonne. Quoted on the Toronto, New York and London Stock Exchanges, the Saskatoon-based **Potash Corporation of Saskatchewan (POT)** is the largest supplier of potash in the world. In 2008 it announced a $400 per tonne increase in sales to China's largest fertiliser distributor, Sinofert, a jump of 230% over 2007 prices. Producing potash from six mines in Saskatchewan and one in New Brunswick, Potash Corporation of Saskatchewan had a market capitalisation of $33 billion by mid-2009, making it one of Canada's most valuable companies. In 2007, its potash production of 9.159 million tons represented 48% of all North American potash production. The company also produces nitrogen fertilisers, nitrogen feed and other industrial products including urea, ammonium nitrate, nitric acid and ammonia, and it has nitrogen facilities in Georgia, Louisiana and Ohio in the US and in Trinidad.

5. The International Energy Agency Sounds the Alarm

Leave oil before it leaves us.

Fatih Birol, IEA Chief Economist, May 2008

Lost in the media melee over the collapse of Lehman Bros in September 2008 and the subsequent international banking crisis, was the publication of the IEA's 2008 'World Energy Outlook', a key report dealing with the world endowment of oil. What is significant about this report is that for the first time the IEA, long a sceptic of peak oil, admitted the validity of some worrying findings and rang the bell on the end of cheap oil, thereby heralding a new economic age. The report marks a watershed in the debate about peak oil, sends alarming signals to national governments and should be compulsory reading for anyone hitherto unconvinced about peak oil.

The IEA is an autonomous body, established in November 1974 within the framework of the Organisation for Economic Co-operation and Development (OECD) to implement an international energy programme. It carries out a programme of energy co-operation among its twenty-eight members, including Ireland and the UK, who between them comprise most of the OECD.

In updating its view on global energy trends, the IEA provides us with an alternative view to that produced by peak oil proponents. In the past, the gap between these two positions has been very wide. That gap is now closing quickly.

Even taking the 'Goldilocks' view that untapped oil resources, such as Canadian oil sands, will come onstream to bridge the widening gap between demand growth and production, the IEA is predicting a severe oil crunch until at least 2015, after which it believes that substantial extra investment in oil and gas infrastructure should rescue the day. The great difficulty with this scenario is its reliance on halting the decline in existing oil production and meeting rising demand by tapping into new sources of oil, most particularly oil sands.

To get oil out of oil sands requires vast quantities of heat, and so, as energy costs rise, so do extraction costs. Remember, there is no point in spending €1 in energy input to get €1 of energy output. This equation has beggared the economics around oil sands to date. The second weakness is the reliance on a very substantial global investment in energy infrastructure which, because of the downturn, is already well behind where it needs to be to match the IEA's forecasts. Even for starry eyed optimists and those who believe in the myths surrounding oil, the IEA report is a wakeup call.

What the IEA report is telling us

The global energy model is at a crossroads. Energy supply and energy consumption are unsustainable – environmentally, socially and economically. Future prosperity is directly linked to how the world tackles the supply of reliable and affordable energy on the one hand and how it moves to a low-carbon, environmentally friendly model on the other. In short, an energy revolution is needed.

The IEA calculates that the primary demand for global energy will grow by 45% from 2006 until 2030, which is an average growth of 1.6% a year, with fossil fuels accounting for 80% of the world's primary energy mix by 2030. Demand growth in non-OECD countries is the principal driver, accounting for 87% of the predicted increase in energy demand over the next twenty years. This means that no matter what energy conservation measures are taken in the developed world, such will be the demand for energy from the developing world that we are locked into a path of ever increasing pressure on oil and fossil fuels. That spells higher prices no matter what else occurs.

In order to maintain existing oil and gas infrastructure and meet exploration and development needs, a total investment of $26.3 trillion will be needed over the next twenty years. Based on existing trends, oil demand of 85 mbpd in 2007 will rise to 106 mbpd by 2030, an average rise of 1% a year. Gas is expected to grow at 1.3% a year and coal at 2% a year, with alternative energy expanding at a much faster rate of 8% annually.

It is demand from the non-OECD regions that will shape the story of oil over the next two decades, with India seeing the fastest growth at 3.9% a year, followed by China at 3.5% a year, but emerging Asian economies and the Middle East are also seeing very high rates of growth. This contrasts with demand growth in OECD regions falling over the same period. By the time we reach 2030, global oil demand in OECD countries will be less than from non-OECD countries, at 43% and 57% of the world market, respectively. Unlike OECD countries, where high excise tax rates dominate oil prices, subsidies are a characteristic of non-OECD countries. In 2007 alone, oil subsidies amounted to $150 billion globally.

Three-quarters of the projected increase in oil demand globally will come from the transport sector and, despite a shift towards greater fuel efficiency, there will be a massive growth in the car fleet globally, rising from an estimated 650 million vehicles in 2005 to 1.4 billion by 2030. Such is the increase in demand growth, and the tightness against supply, the IEA estimates that oil spending, which has soared from 1% of global GDP in 1999 to 4% in 2007, will stabilise at 5% of GDP over the next twenty years, but that spending will be higher in non-OECD countries, settling down somewhere between 6% and 7% of GDP.

The IEA maintains that global oil production will not reach peak before 2030, but it is basing its assumption on a large net increase in oil production coming from natural gas liquids and from Canadian oil sands. The world will become more, not less, reliant on OPEC countries, whose market share will rise from 44% in 2007 to 51% by 2030. Saudi Arabia will remain the largest oil producer in the world: the IEA estimates its output will climb from 10.2 mbpd in 2007 to 15.6 mbpd in 2030. Oil production is already levelling off in non-OPEC regions and is projected to decline from around 2015.

Based on this scenario, the IEA estimates that the world's endowment of oil will be large enough to support the market, but this is entirely dependent on natural gas liquids and the controversial Canadian oil sands, as well as on a very substantial increase in investment in oil and gas infrastructure and in exploration and development. As its report points out, however, there is no guarantee that these resources will be exploited quickly enough to offset the declining rate of production in existing oil fields.

As noted in the Introduction, the IEA calculates that four new Saudi Arabias would need to be discovered just to keep up with present demand. If no new supplies were to come on stream over the next twenty years there would be a gap of 45 mbpd of gross capacity – a little over half the current production. Of course, there will be some new supplies, but even the additional 23 mbpd which the IEA expects to be produced by 2015 will fall short of predicted demand by around 7 mbpd. In short, the IEA is estimating an oil crunch by 2015 because net oil-production capacity is expected to tail off after 2010 and more capacity is unlikely to be met because of the underinvestment resulting from the current worldwide financial crisis.

Basing its overall model on the requirement to spend $26 trillion (in 2007 terms), half of which will be needed simply to maintain the current global infrastructure for supplying oil, gas, coal and electricity, the IEA calculates that oil will double in price in nominal terms to $200 per barrel by 2030, or $120 in today's terms. Unlike the most recent oil crisis from 1973 to 1983, national oil companies will dominate the next one, accounting for 80% of extra production in both oil and gas over the next two decades.

The IEA model hinges on adequate and timely investment and on Canadian oil sands coming on stream. When demand growth is taken into account, some 64 mbpd of additional gross capacity will be needed; that's six times what Saudi Arabia produces today. There remains a real risk that the investment will not arrive on time or in sufficient volume to avoid a severe oil-supply crunch over the next two decades. In its scenario, the IEA is hoping that recoverable oil resources, which include initial proven and probable reserves from discovered fields, reserved growth and oil that is yet to be found (estimated at 3.5 trillion barrels) will do the trick, pointing out that only a third of this total, or 1.1 trillion barrels, has been produced up until now.

Undiscovered resources account for about a third of the predicted remaining recoverable oil, mostly lying in the Middle East, Russia and the Caspian region. Non-conventional oil resources, from oil sands and extra-heavy oil, estimated at between 1 and 2 trillion barrels of oil and concentrated mostly in Alberta, Canada, and in the Orinoco Belt in Venezuela, may ultimately be recoverable economically. When these are added to the pot, along with coal-to-liquids and gas-to-liquids, the potential is for about 9 trillion barrels. In 2008 three countries – Russia, Iran and Qatar – held 56% of the world's reserves and twenty-five fields worldwide held almost half of this.

The IEA is realistic in emphasising repeatedly that there can be no guarantee that these fields will be exploited quickly enough to meet the rising level of demand, particularly from non-OECD countries. The increasing dominance of national oil companies poses a risk to the required investment being made as resource-rich countries focus on slowing their depletion rates of natural resources. One way or the other, the next two decades will see much higher oil prices with a substantial risk that shortages could occur.

Parallel impact of CO_2 emissions

In order to meet the economic expansion of the non-OECD world, it is already clear that there will be a very substantial increase in energy consumption over the next twenty years, exacerbating greenhouse gas emissions and raising global temperatures. Unless adjusted, this has the potential for catastrophic and irreversible climate change. Without change in government policies, we are on track to double the concentration of greenhouse gases in the atmosphere to 1,000 parts per million (ppm) of CO_2 by the end of this century, increasing global temperatures by an unsustainable 6°C.

Even in the short term, CO_2 emissions are projected to rise from 28 billion tonnes in 2006 to 41 billion by 2030. That's an increase of 45%.

A whopping 75% of the projected increase in CO_2 emissions will arise from China, India and the Middle East, and 97% from the non-OECD countries when taken as a whole. Europe and Japan are the only areas where emissions are expected to be lower in 2030 than they are today. Unsurprisingly, the power generation and transport sectors will contribute 70% of the projected increase in CO_2 emissions by 2030.

The 2009 UN conference on climate change in Copenhagen, which hoped to establish an international framework of action on CO_2 emissions, had its work cut out. Three-quarters of the projected total output of electricity by 2020 and more than half of it by 2030 will come from power stations that are already operating today and that do not contain the technology to reduce CO_2 emissions. Based on its model of future energy demand growth, and where the energy sector accounts for 61% of global greenhouse gas emissions, very strong action will be needed within an international framework to tackle CO_2.

The IEA has examined two targets for lowering greenhouse gas emissions. This means stabilising emissions to either 550 ppm, in which case temperatures rise by an extra 3°C, or stabilising them at 450ppm, in which case temperatures rise by 2°C. The solution will require a mixture of cap-and-trade systems, sectoral agreements and national measures if these targets are to be met. The IEA points out that, to meet the targets, there needs to be a very significant shift in the energy mix, requiring much more investment in energy-related infrastructure and equipment.

Global energy investment over the next twenty years will need to be $4.1 trillion higher than currently expected, or an extra 0.25% of annual world GDP, to meet the less severe target of 550ppm. In order to meet the harder target of 450ppm, extra global energy investment of $9.3 trillion will be required, or an additional 0.55% of annual GDP.

So, what does all this mean?

If you want to simplify matters, the IEA model is the best-case scenario, i.e. the 'Goldilocks' model. This estimates that peak oil will occur around 2030, but that is based on a set of assumptions that are highly vulnerable to being blown off course. It is banking on very substantial investment in energy infrastructure, continuing co-operation from national oil companies in a mutually interdependent global energy market that is not interrupted by geopolitical shocks, and also assumes better economics, particularly for non-conventional sources such as Canadian oil sands. If all that happens – and it is a big 'if' – we can still expect very substantial increases in oil prices and we can say with absolute certainty that there will be an oil crunch until at least 2015. That's the optimistic scenario.

The pessimistic scenario put forward by peak oil analysts is that we are already past the peak and that it occurred around 2005 to 2008. These analysts argue that the increase in oil prices before the global downturn in 2008, when oil hit $147 a barrel, is more likely to indicate the fundamental price of oil. In the pessimistic scenario, the investment and infrastructure will not arrive in time, nor will non-conventional sources or new explorations become feasible at prices which the market will be able to bear.

But, wherever you pitch your tent between these two models, there is the parallel issue of CO_2 emissions. The scenario from the IEA does not take account of the substantial change in the global energy mix needed to take us off the trajectory of global temperatures rising by 6°C during this century. The UN framework on climate change, advanced in 2009 in Copenhagen, will perhaps produce some form of agreement that will have an impact on the world energy market, but which will require substantial extra spending as a percentage of world GDP in order to meet the targets set.

Whichever way you slice and dice it, we are entering the Age of Scarcity in which the relative cost of energy is going to dominate economics. Remember, oil isn't the only natural resource of the planet that is approaching peak and coming under pressure as a consequence of the substantial growth in the global economy.

What we can say with absolute certainty is that the era of cheap oil is over, even though price volatility will remain a feature. Current energy trends are unsustainable, national oil companies are in the ascendancy and very substantial investment is needed to offset oil-field decline rates. UN conferences on climate change will need to deliver a post-2012 climate change regime that works. Not only will massive investment be required to meet these problems, but it will need to be matched by enormous technological breakthroughs, for example in clean-coal capture. The economic age that we are entering is vastly different from the one we are leaving, heralded by the credit-bubble burst of 2008, so it's best to consign the conventions that have dominated our lives up until now to history and adapt to the new economic age emerging.

6. Understanding Oil

Oil

How much do you know about oil? Be honest. It just kind of appears, doesn't it, at the end of the hose when you fill your car. You don't even have to handle the lousy stuff, thankfully, because it smells to high heaven and would ruin your perfume or aftershave. OK, you read about it occasionally, but only when prices rise, then it gets a few minutes from talking heads on the main news squeezed somewhere between trouble flaring at the end of an Old Firm derby in Glasgow and a burned-out celebrity going into rehab. If you are anything like I used to be, you're probably pretty clueless about petrochemicals, too, despite the fact that our lives revolve around access to them at prices we can afford. You probably don't even know how oil was formed and how much of it is left. No need to feel foolish, I hadn't a clue either until I read about it for the first time.

Where oil comes from

Decomposing organic matter over millions of years produced oil when underground heat of up to 150°C kick-started the process of changing it into hydrocarbons, which come in different degrees of complexity from the simple mixture of one carbon atom and four hydrogen atoms to make methane – CH_4 – to the larger chains of atoms required to make crude oil.

Over millions of years, much of the oil bubbled through to the surface and bio-degraded. The remaining 10% or so held in underground reserves has been producing the oil that has fuelled the modern economy since the first well was drilled in Pennsylvania in 1859. If you'd like to get a revealing insight into the baby steps of the small independent oil-drilling industry in the early twentieth century as oil began to overtake coal as the dominant source of energy, rent a copy of the Oscar-winning film *There Will Be Blood*. The movie provides a remarkable insight into the early oil business and produces an extraordinary performance by Daniel Day-Lewis as an oil-obsessed independent well-owner competing against John Rockefeller's Standard Oil, which would later be broken up by the US Department of Justice to become Exxon, Mobil, Chevron (previously Standard of California) and Marathon Oil.

Peakers

In 1956 a leading US physicist, Dr Marion King Hubbert (1903–89), predicted that the US would reach peak oil production in 1970. In making this prediction he drew widespread derision from critics, but he was proved entirely accurate as US reserves started to decline just before the 1970s oil crisis. Hubbert used a bell curve to explain how, after extracting the easy oil, the total level of production would inevitably decline, making it more and more difficult to extract oil at reasonable prices. His model was later extended to look at peak oil as a global phenomenon.

In more recent years, Dr Colin Campbell, who, like Hubbert, has also faced derision from critics, founded ASPO, the Association for the Study of Peak Oil and Gas. ASPO started as a network of European scientists and others who had a keen interest in determining the date at which peak oil would be reached and when the world's production of oil and gas would begin to decline due to natural resource constraints. ASPO's mission is threefold: firstly, to evaluate and define the world's endowment of oil and gas; secondly, to study depletion, taking account of economic demand, technology and politics; and, thirdly, to raise awareness of the serious consequences of the oil and gas decline for mankind.

The ASPO model is a dynamic one that is updated regularly with any new information about oil and gas reserves throughout the world. Figures 6.1 to 6.4 show the latest position of the model, reproduced with the kind permission of ASPO, which estimates that peak oil occurred in 2005 (6.1). Coincidentally, it was just after this period that oil prices (6.4) began to escalate at a rapid rate, before the severe economic contraction in late 2008 and 2009 drove it under $40 a barrel. By 2010 oil was back up trading at $70–$80 a barrel and poised to go higher as global economic recovery strengthened demand, especially from non-OECD countries. Peaks happen at different times in different regions. The peak happened in the United States in 1970, as predicted by Dr Hubbert. The peak in Europe was in 1999 and in Russia in 1987. Peak is estimated to have occurred in the Middle East and Gulf region in 1974 and it occurred in the rest of the world in 2005. The model also takes account of potential flows from deepwater oil fields, polar fields, etc., putting peak dates for these, including gas, at times ranging from 2013 to 2030 (6.2). As noted elsewhere, overall production continues to trend upward to satisfy increasing demand, despite the fact that very little new easily extractable oil remains to be discovered (6.3).

How much oil is left?

Given their levels of transparency in government, there is no reason to doubt the reserves declared by countries such as the

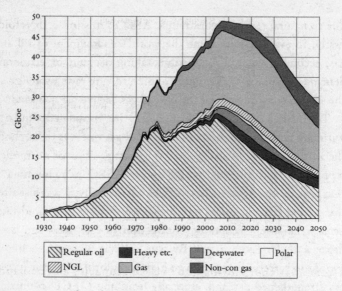

Figure 6.1 Oil and gas production profiles – 2008 base case

ESTIMATED PRODUCTION TO 2100										
Amount		Gb	Annual Production – Regular Oil						Total	Peak
Regular Oil			Mb/d	2008	2010	2015	2020	2030	Gb	Date
Past	Future	Total	US-48	2.9	2.6	2.1	1.7	1.1	200	1970
Known Fields	New		Europe	4.0	3.5	2.5	1.8	0.9	75	1999
1054	736	110	1900	Russia	8.8	8.2	6.8	5.7	4.0	230	1987
846			ME Gulf	20	20	20	19	16	673	1974
All Liquids			Other	28	27	23	19	14	722	2005
1156	1269	2425	World	64	61	54	47	36	1900	2005
2008 Base Scenario			Non-Conventional							
Regular Oil excludes Heavy Oils			Heavy etc.	4.3	5.0	6.5	7.2	7.7	226	2030
(inc. tarsands oilshales) Polar &			Deepwater	5.9	6.6	8.1	8.1	4.7	89	2013
Deepwater Oil; & gasplant NGL			Polar	1.4	1.5	1.7	2.0	2.3	52	2030
and Refinery Gains of ~3%			Gas Liquid	5.1	5.5	5.6	5.9	5.6	156	2020
Reference date: end 2008			*Rounding*			−1		−1	2	
Revised 10/03/2009			All	81	80	75	70	55	2425	2008

Figure 6.2 The growing gap between past and estimated future discoveries

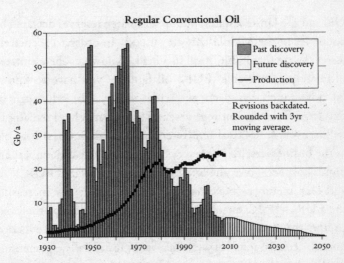

Figure 6.3 The growing gap between capacity and demand

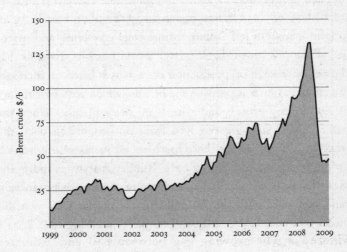

Figure 6.4 The price of oil, 1999–2009

UK and the United States, but the estimated reserves declared by countries in the Middle East are suspect. In order to accurately assess the total amount of oil in a field – known as the estimated ultimately recoverable (EUR) oil figure – you have to know: (a) how much has been extracted already; (b) what can be extracted from current reserves; and (c) how much oil remains to be discovered. Political interference in the oil business is as old as the business itself. The reserves stated by OPEC members are highly suspect, given the link between their declared EUR level and each member's maximum production quota. By increasing the EUR, OPEC members can increase their slice of the cake. In the 1980s, as OPEC members squabbled over production quotas, declared reserves were increased substantially – sometimes doubling or trebling in an instant – without any major new discoveries.

Already some analysts examining OPEC's EURs reckon that they are exaggerated by about 14% and these analysts reduce its total EUR of 2,138 billion barrels to 1,888 billion barrels. In an insightful analysis Jeff Rubin, former chief economist and strategist at the investment bank CIBC World Markets, reckons that the net increase in oil production since 2005 is based on increases in natural gas such as propane and butane, which are a by-product of the drilling process and arise as oil fields mature. When the natural gas liquids are removed from oil production data, the stark conclusion is that there has been no increase in crude-oil production since the end of 2005. Rubin's analysis supports the view that peak oil may be happening now. So long as production can't keep pace with the demand that is rising at 4% a year, oil prices will rise. Rubin estimates oil prices reaching over $200 a barrel by 2012.

Oil exports cut to meet domestic demand

Another major factor impinging on rising oil prices is the demand growth from within oil-producing nations themselves who, at the current rate of trajectory, will combine to become the second largest users of oil in the world outside of the United States. Petrol in mid-2008 was selling for a mere 25 cents a gallon in Venezuela and between 50 and 60 cents in other oil-producing countries like Iran, Saudi Arabia and Kuwait. Prices at these levels attract high increases in consumption in home markets. In Russia, where the car fleet increased by a massive 60% in 2007, exports are set to decline, adding further tightness to international supply. Mexico

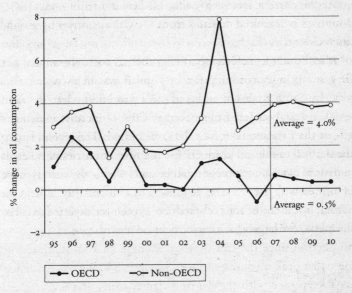

Figure 6.5 Two very different consumption trends for oil

Source: Jeff Rubin, CIBC World Markets, ASPO Annual Conference, City Hall Cork, 2007.

is facing a rapid depletion, at a rate of 15% a year, at its giant Cantarell oil field, cutting into its exports to the US and removing Mexico entirely from the export market by 2012.

Oil-producing nations will feed their own population's energy demands first, restricting the amount of oil available for export at a time when demand is rising rapidly, especially from non-OECD countries and from China, which is on course to become the world's largest oil consumer. Efficiency drives in developed countries, which have depressed demand growth to 0.5% annually, are a contributing factor, subsidising prices in non-OECD countries where demand growth is eight times higher at 4% a year. Figure 6.5 charts these two differing trends.

At the current rate of growth, oil demand from non-OECD countries will exceed demand from OECD countries by around 2017. Countries that have access to cheap oil will use larger amounts of it and use it less efficiently. From 2001 to 2006, the annual rate of growth in oil consumption by Kuwait was in excess of 7% a year, by Saudi Arabia in excess of 5% a year and by Iran in excess of 4% a year, compared to an average OECD increase in demand of less than 1% annually over the same period. The second largest users of oil in the world are OPEC member countries plus Russia and Mexico, where combined total demand will shortly touch 15 mbpd compared with the US at more than 20 to 21 mbpd. Just around the corner, by the end of 2010, oil-producer exports are expected to fall by 2.5 mbpd, due largely to domestic demand growth.

The skewed barrels

Ideally, the supply of any commodity should be fragmented and well spread out, rather than skewed in favour of a small number of mega-reserves, so that if a few sources tap-out, others can take up the slack. Unfortunately, global oil supplies are heavily dependent on a small number of elephant fields. A colossal 50% of all oil produced comes from just 3% of all fields. When a small oil field passes peak, it has little impact on world oil prices. When a giant oil field passes peak, it can have a big effect. Fourteen of the world's elephant oil fields have been exploited on average for more than forty-four years. Decline in an oil field is expected on average after fifty years.

Here's how the global barrel is skewed:

Just fourteen fields, each pumping more than half a million barrels of oil per day and averaging 993,000 barrels, are responsible for 20% of global production.

Twelve fields produce between 300,000 and 500,000 barrels per day, 6% of global production.

Twenty-nine fields produce between 200,000 and 300,000 barrels per day, 9% of global production.

Sixty-one fields produce between 100,000 and 200,000 barrels per day, 12% of global production.

More than 4,000 small fields produce on average just 9,000 barrels per day and combine to account for 53% of global production.

When is peak?

What is clear is that a significant decline in output from the very big fields, particularly the four largest, would cause a severe tension between supply and demand and rapidly accelerate oil price rises. We know that three of these four mega-fields have already passed peak and are in decline: Cantarell in Mexico, Burgan in

Kuwait and Daqing in China. In addition, the fifty-year-old Ghawar mega-field in Saudi Arabia may also be past peak, but it's hard to know for certain because of the lack of transparency in Saudi reports. This is a critical point because, if Ghawar is past peak – and some analysts think Ghawar is over two-thirds depleted – then the estimate of peak oil having occurred in 2005 looks more accurate. Ghawar, which produces 50% of Saudi oil, is now being pumped with sea water to maintain pressure levels, a process that wouldn't be required unless the world's largest oil field was in decline. But whether the ASPO projection of peak oil in 2005 is correct remains a moot point.

In a study undertaken by Dr Samuel Foucher on the projections of nineteen oil analysts, a remarkable consensus on peak oil was found, with most estimating it as occurring between 2009 and 2012. We already know that a number of major players such as the United States, Norway, Indonesia and the United Kingdom, shortly to be followed by China, are past their geological peak for oil production. For various reasons, including underinvestment in infrastructure, Russia, Mexico and Kuwait are following. Moreover, Russia, Mexico, Iran and Venezuela will soon be selling more oil within their borders than they will be exporting and the supply from non-OPEC countries has been flat since 2001 and that is unlikely to change.

All roads lead to Saudi Arabia in the hope that the Saudis can increase global production by opening the tap and pumping more oil. Officially, OPEC's view is that there isn't a problem with crude-oil supply, the problem is with underinvestment in refining. This may go some way to explaining why, sensing that their region is once again in control of world oil markets, the Middle Eastern countries, which dominate OPEC, are pumping $310 billion down the distribution chain into refining, but, tellingly, investing 82% less into the tap that would expand oil production capacity.

Future oil demand

As the world economy grows, its demand for energy rises and, hence, oil consumption increases. Taking both OECD and non-OECD countries together, the average rate of increase in demand had been 1.5% a year; however, this jumped to 2% in 2007. Global oil demand, currently hovering between 85 and 87 mbpd, is expected to increase to 120 mbpd by 2030. Much as the widening of a motorway simply encourages more traffic and more congestion, energy-efficiency drives in OECD countries will simply increase usage of oil elsewhere.

The link between population growth and oil consumption is pretty clear. A decline in oil production, unless it is bridged with renewable energy, will have an impact on population growth. The two most populated countries in the world, China and India, are both experiencing tiger economic growth of 7% to 9% a year. This rate of growth is unsustainable without a corresponding spectacular increase in energy supply.

When you consider that a 5% increase in mobile phone usage in China is equivalent to a 40% increase in the US marketplace, you get an idea of the impact of growth in demand in China for just about anything. The estimated annual increase in oil consumption for China is 5% between now and 2015 and this may be an underestimate. China, which already consumes 10% of the world's energy, will need to import two-thirds of its energy in order to feed this economic momentum. Developing countries are expected to account for 80% of the growth in world energy demand to 2020 – and a third of that growth is attributable to China, which, with a population four times that of the US, would need to record a tenfold increase in oil consumption to reach the Western standard of living it desires.

China's rapid growth is also having an effect on other sources of energy, including coal, for which demand is growing at a rate of 14% per year. Chinese appetite for coal accounts for 75% of world demand growth.

The Chinese car fleet increased by 25% in 2007, but with fewer than 30 million cars on its roads, the scope for growth in car ownership in China is vast. China will need an additional 11.7 million barrels of oil per day to meet the demand from the additional 120 million cars expected on its roads over the next ten years. The IEA reckons that the Chinese car fleet will expand to 270 million by 2030. India is little different with a population of 1.1 billion and an average economic growth rate of 8%. In 2007, the car fleet in India expanded by 25% in the year which also saw the launch of the new budget car, the Tata Nano, by Indian tycoon Ratan Tata, a compact selling for just $2,500.

Given the limit to oil production, increases in the millions of new motorists in India and China will probably be paid for by a fall in the number of drivers in OECD countries. As petrol touches $4 a gallon in the US and nearly double that in Europe, where fossil-fuel taxes are higher, rail traffic is already on the increase (see investing in railways, page 154).

Despite representing just 4.5% of the world's population, the United States, with a population of 300 million, is the largest consumer of energy on the planet and it imports two-thirds of its oil. The US total demand for oil at nearly 21 mbpd represents 25% of the world's oil consumption. US oil consumption is expected to fall by over 2 mbpd by 2012 when gas prices are forecast to hit $7 a gallon, halving the number of miles a motorist, at 2007 prices, could travel on a dollar's worth of petrol and leading to a wholesale switch to economy cars, accelerated by US government demand for reform from its battered auto-manufacturing giants.

Meanwhile, back at the ranch, Ireland's daft transport policy harshly exposes the Irish economy, having given primacy to road building for the past ten years rather than to developing high-speed rail links. In 2008, more than 90% of commercial loads were carried by road hauliers with the rail commercial market share continuing to decline. Although there has been some investment in rail, passenger traffic has simply matched population growth and railway stations lack the capacity to expand to include adequate park-and-ride facilities due to land prices and a dearth of integrated thinking in long-term transport planning. Irish transport policy remains lamentable, based as it is on the discredited and outdated assumption that oil prices will be at about $100 per barrel by 2020.

Global demand, then, currently at up to 87 mbpd, is on track to reach 120 mbpd by 2030 based on current demand growth rates. But that rate of expansion would require the discovery of several new mega-fields on a scale that would make Saudi reserves look like a puddle. Let's face it: it's not going to happen. Whichever way you look at it, there won't be enough oil to meet increased demand. Nobody knows for certain just how high oil prices will go. Much of it will depend on the impact of rising oil prices on demand and there remains the ever-present and catastrophic risk of Israeli or US military confrontation with Iran, which threatens to block the strategic Strait of Hormuz and cut off Middle East oil shipments, 60% of world supply (see Figure 6.6, overleaf).

Oil sands

Canada is seen as the great saviour by oil enthusiasts. Canada has the world's most extensive oil sands, estimated by some to be capable of producing 2.5 trillion barrels of oil! Sound too good to be

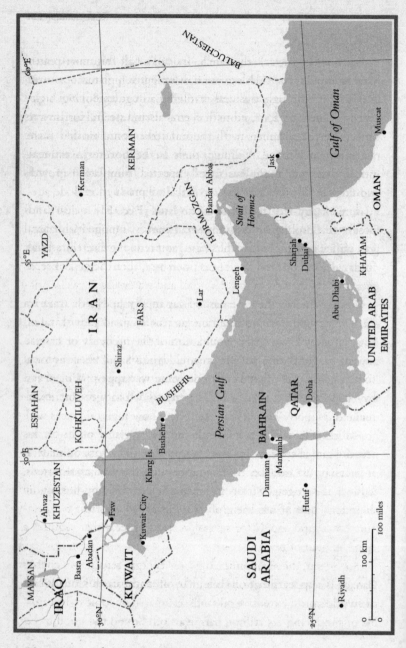

Figure 6.6 The Strait of Hormuz

true? It is. Oil (or tar) sands are a mix of asphalt (bitumen), earth, sand and water. Asphalt does not flow except at high temperatures. Refining it is an ugly business involving a huge amount of strip-mining. The sand is mixed with chemicals and steam in giant vats to bubble the bitumen to the top and the contaminated waste water is then dumped into huge ponds. In the short term, and realistically, the maximum level of oil expected from Canadian sands would probably add about 1% to global oil production.

The energy return on energy invested (EROEI) for oil sands poses a real problem. Vast amounts of energy, supplied by natural gas, are needed to produce the steam required to free up the asphalt from the clay and sand. So, as gas prices rise, then the cost of separating the asphalt from the clay, sand and water rises as well. Analysts question whether the natural gas supply in North America will be sufficient to supply the energy to lift Canadian tar-sand oil to 3 mbpd by 2025. Only about a fifth of the oil sands are easy to access. The rest are small, fragmented deposits and uneconomical to mine. Massive amounts of toxic waste water are produced as a by-product, which may take 200 years to detoxify in vast, man-made lakes.

Oil shale is similar to oil sands and the largest deposits of this resource are in the United States. To get bitumen from oil shale, it is necessary to free the mixture of organic chemical compounds, known as kerogen, within the rock. This is done by putting an electrical current into the ground to heat the rocks to a temperature of around 370°C for several years, a process that requires a huge amount of energy.

So, given the economic logic of energy return on energy invested, it appears that oil shale, like oil sands, are dubious at best as solutions.

Natural gas and coal

It stands to reason that as energy demand grows and oil prices rise, so too will the price of gas and coal. It's hard to believe but, in the early days of oil production, natural gas was burned off rather than used. Much like oil, natural gas faces its own peak, albeit a little later, based on the ASPO model. Three countries dominate the world's gas reserves: Russia, 27%; Iran, 16%; and Qatar 15%. Saudi Arabia and the United States have 4%; Nigeria, United Arab Emirates, Venezuela and Algeria each have 3%; Indonesia and Iraq have 2% each. In natural gas production terms, the United States is higher up the list and is second to Russia, which produces the most at 23% of global gas supply while the United States produces 19%. Just like the oil story, and despite extra drilling, new gas wells are smaller and have less high-energy gas than those already in production.

Coal provides about 25% of the total energy demand of the world and 40% of its electricity. China is responsible for over one-third of coal consumption with the US coming next at 10% and India at 7%.

While the volume of coal production is increasing, the overall energy content is declining, as less high-energy anthracite is mined, and the cost of transporting coal is rising as oil prices go up. Estimates of coal reserves are greatly out of date and highly unreliable. In recent reassessments, both Germany and the UK reduced their coal reserve estimates by 90%. Energy Watch Group, a German consultancy firm, updated reserves for all of the major coal-producing nations and adjusted national reserves downwards, in some cases by 60%, putting peak coal around 2020. Traditional studies have not taken account of the rapid acceleration in coal use as oil and gas depletes. We already know that China has burned up 20% of her coal reserves.

Global coal reserves stand at a little over 900 billion tons, half of which is low-grade coal and 90% of which is located in just six countries: South Africa, Australia, the United States, India, China and Russia. Coal is the dirtiest of the fossil fuels with the highest CO_2 emissions, the environmental cost of which has led to investment in clean-coal technology to capture and store the carbon emissions produced when it is burned. Another embryonic technology currently in development aims to convert coal into a liquid synthetic fuel.

China is, by a long stretch, the most coal-dependent large economy in the world. As a result, it emits twice as much carbon per unit of energy than Europe and it plans to commission another 500 coal-burning power plants by 2012. It's not the only developing country to embark on aggressive expansion of coal burning; populous countries like Indonesia and Vietnam are following suit. Meanwhile, developed nations like the US and other OECD countries are committing to aggressive emission cuts. It's simply economically unsustainable for businesses in OECD countries to absorb the cost of carbon emissions while facing competition from low-cost countries that are manufacturing goods without carbon costs. Ultimately, Europe and the US, as it follows Obama's green policies, will be forced to apply carbon tariffs on imports that have been manufactured with dirty energy that is free of carbon emission costs. Lower carbon emission costs will begin to counter lower-cost labour as manufacturing begins to migrate back to countries that enjoy carbon advantage, a process that will accelerate as carbon emission costs ramp up from their current level. The result should see countries like China and India going green quickly, not just to protect exports but also from the mounting evidence of alarming water shortages as the availability of melting ice water reduces with the thinning of Himalayan glaciers.

Investing

Oil and fossil fuels

Each year we are finding less high-quality crude oil, natural gas and coal and we are paying more to exploit it. Meanwhile, energy demand is rising. Last time round, in the 1970s, money invested in the oil majors outperformed inflation by nearly 7% a year. This time, it's different. The big integrated oil companies have left their best days behind them as their reserves continue to shrink. Don't be fooled by the mega-profits that have been made over recent years. The oil majors will be squeezed by the national oil companies and will be forced into continuous mergers to stay in the game. The lightbulb on declining oil reserves has yet to go on in Wall Street and in London but, when it does, you don't want to be holding shares in the oil majors.

The conventional approach to investing in oil is to invest in what are called the oil majors, companies like ExxonMobil, Total BP, Royal Dutch Shell, Chevron, etc. Investors can do this directly by picking them or indirectly by investing in ETFs that cover the oil majors and oil refiners. You'll find a range of different ways to play the oil market, such as the **ETFS Dow Jones STOXX 600 Oil & Gas Fund (London: OILS)**, but, be warned, thirteen of the largest oil-producing businesses in the world are national oil companies. As oil depletes, it is likely that these government-owned oil companies will dominate the market and the value of publicly quoted oil-production companies will fall. There are a plethora of exchange-traded commodities that provide opportunities to invest in oil futures, including using leverage, but there are more focused ways to invest by concentrating on companies with strong stories to tell.

PETROBRAS

One of my favourite companies is an exception, **Petrobras (NYSE: PBR)**, a multi award-winning Brazilian oil, gas and biofuel producer that's poised to throw off lots of cash over the years ahead. With a market capitalisation in mid-2009 at a chunky $180 billion Petrobras (Petroleo Brasileiro), which began its operation in Brazil in 1954, is the largest publicly traded oil company in Latin America. Petrobras operates in the exploration, production, refining, trading and transportation of crude oil, oil products, natural gas and other fluid hydrocarbons. It has just found a new oil field with potential recoverable oil reserves of between 700 million and 1 billion barrels, increasing its huge pool of oil reserves to 9.6 billion barrels, which is similar to those held by the giant Conoco Phillips.

In addition to its massive oil reserves, Petrobras is one of the largest players in alternative energy. Brazil has had a head start and has been actively engaged in becoming oil independent since the 1970s. Nearly half of the Brazilian car fleet is part-fuelled with Petrobras biofuel, which is now also exported to other countries, including the United States, India and Japan. Petrobras has committed to spend $54 billion on its biofuel and oil production and on its distribution facilities to 2011. In mid-2009, trading at nearly ten times earnings, compared to twenty-five times earnings in early 2008, it has plenty of momentum as oil and gas prices rise and it continues to be the world's biggest producer of biofuel, a renewable fuel stock that will increase in importance as fossil fuels deplete.

Petrobras will gain from rising oil prices and the continuing switch towards biofuels, but what about natural gas? For that, take a look at EnCana.

ENCANA

Natural gas giant **EnCana Corporation (NYSE: ECA)** provides an opportunity to invest in the natural gas market and is the largest independent gas producer and operator in North America, as well as having its own oil interests. EnCana is a huge landowner in North America, holding 25 million acres and owning 18.9 trillion cubic feet of proven gas reserves with a ten-year drilling pipeline on its existing developed lands. With headquarters in Calgary in Alberta, Canada, EnCana employs 7,250 people across the United States and Canada and was created by the merger of Pan-Canadian Energy Corporation (PCE) and Alberta Energy Corporation Ltd (AEC) in April 2002. EnCana had a market capitalisation in mid-2009 of nearly $40 billion, selling at approximately six times its earnings, compared to fifteen times earnings during the energy peak price in 2008.

SERVICE COMPANIES

In the 1970s, oil service companies made lots of cash. This time round, they stand to do so again, even if the oil majors are facing market shrinkage. Perhaps one of the best positioned as the competition to get at harder-to-exploit, high-quality oil heats up is **Transocean (NYSE: RIG)**, because it's the world's largest deep-sea oil driller. Transocean has approximately seventy floating rigs and sixty-five jack-ups in its fleet with nine new-build ultra-deepwater floaters expected to be operational from the middle of 2009 to 2011. With a market capitalisation of $24 billion in mid-2009, Transocean, together with its subsidiaries, provides offshore drilling services for oil and gas wells, specialising in deepwater and harsh-environment drilling services. Transocean has been rein-vesting cash flows into expanding its ultra-deepwater rig fleet and is one of my favourite stocks because deepwater drilling is in a strong up cycle. Holding Transocean in combination with Petrobras and EnCana makes for a good mix in this sector, but other service companies will also do well.

Noble Corporation (NYSE: NE), with a market capitalisation of $8 billion in mid-2009, is another major offshore drilling company. Founded in 1921, Noble Corporation has become one of the largest offshore drilling contractors in the world and has a fleet of sixty-two mobile offshore drilling units located in the US, the Middle East, the Gulf of Mexico, the North Sea, Brazil, West Africa and India. It has five new rigs under construction and is clearly investing in further expansion as the race begins for more oil.

Weatherford International Ltd (NYSE: WFT) is valued at circa $14 billion and employs approximately 40,000 in more than 100 countries, with eighty-seven manufacturing facilities supporting 730 service bases. The company provides a full range of services from drilling through to evaluation, completion and production and intervention.

The giant in the operation services sector is **Schlumberger Ltd (NYSE: SLB)**. With a market capitalisation at $64 billion, Schlumberger was trading in mid-2009 at thirteen times earnings and is the leading oil-field services provider worldwide for both the oil and gas industries, employing over 80,000 people in operations across eighty countries. In 2007 Schlumberger committed $728 million to research and development. Founded in 1933 by brothers Marcel and Conrad Schlumberger, the company has generations of experience in providing full-package support services, including monitoring seismic studies for exploration companies.

REFINERS

Another way to play on the race for oil is to invest downstream in the refining business, especially in the largest petrol-consuming market in the world – the USA. These are companies that take crude oil and refine it into end products. Regardless of where the oil is sourced, independent refiners, much like service companies, stand to do handsomely over the times ahead.

This market can be played safely by investing in a huge independent refining company, like **Valero Energy Corporation (NYSE: VLO)**, a Fortune 500 company that commenced operation on 1 January 1980 and is based in San Antonio, Texas, and incorporated in Delaware. Valued by the market at circa $11 billion in mid-2009, Valero employs 22,000 people across North America, has a refining capacity of approximately 3.1 mbpd and has 5,800 retail stores in the United States, Canada and the Caribbean under various brands including Valero, Diamond Shamrock, Shamrock, Ultramar and Beacon.

Tesoro (NYSE: TSO) is the second biggest heavy-crude oil refiner in North America and was capitalised at circa $2.4 billion in mid-2009. Tesoro has its headquarters in San Antonio, Texas, and employs 5,500 people. Through its subsidiaries, the company operates seven refineries in the United States with a combined crude-oil capacity of circa 660,000 barrels per day. It has more than 900 branded retail stations across the United States and was founded in 1968.

One of the most interesting wild cards in this sector is lightweight **SulphCo Inc. (AMEX: SUF)**. Its market capitalisation in mid-2009 was just $100 million, but it specialises in petroleum desulphurisation, a valuable process that improves oil quality by removing the sulphur using high-powered ultrasonic sound waves. This process makes crude oil less dense, allowing more light crude to be recovered during refining while lowering the sulphur content and thus improving the fuel efficiency. In May 2008 SulphCo raised an additional $27.2 million through a combination of an equity placement and a warrant exercise, an investment to scale up its operation to meet anticipated demand for SulphCo's Sono-cracking technology, which is getting a thorough testing through a joint venture between Sulphco and the government of Fujairah in the United Arab Emirates. This joint venture is expected to process 210,000 barrels of oil per day.

The plant aims to provide commercial validation for the Sono-cracking processing and, according to SulphCo, the results to date confirm that the technology makes oil 'less gooey', i.e. it improves the oil's gravity, as measured by the American Petroleum Institute (API) scale, by up to three points. Light crude is defined as having an API gravity higher than 31.3, with medium oil between 22.3 and 31.3, and heavy oil having an API gravity below 22.3. If SulphCo's technology continues to prove successful, and as pressure tightens for higher energy returns from mature oil fields, the growth potential of the company could be very strong.

FUEL FROM COAL

Coal remains a dominant fossil-fuel supply in many parts of the world. Technology designed to create liquids from coal was first developed by Germans in the 1920s and it was further developed by the Nazis during the Second World War when output from synthetic fuel increased substantially. Today, **Sasol (NYSE: SSL)**, the sponsor of the Springboks, South Africa's national rugby squad, is the largest synthetic fuel producer in the world and was valued by the market in mid-2009 at $23 billion. With headquarters in Johannesburg, South Africa, and established in 1950 by the South African government, Sasol manufactures fuels and chemicals from indigenous raw materials. It has developed a technology for the commercial production of synthetic fuels and chemicals from low-grade coal, as well as the conversion of natural gas to environmentally friendly fuels and chemicals. Sasol has 30,000 employees and produces 40% of South Africa's liquid fuel requirements. In addition, the company has substantial chemical assets such as polymers, solvents and fertilisers.

7. Nuclear Power and Hydropower

Long before the world started to think 'green', nuclear power and hydropower had become important players in the energy mix. Unsurprisingly, river-rich countries like Norway are strong in hydropower, but you might be surprised to learn that France leads the world in nuclear power. Nuclear power is concentrated in a relatively small number of countries, but contributes heavily to local markets. The nuclear market is reviving, but not without very serious challenges both to uranium supply and to the environment, which is vulnerable to the long-term effects of nuclear waste. Hydropower, also a mature sector, is harvested by countries rich in hydropower potential, but it is also growing in China and India with both South America and Africa also having substantial hydropower potential. Hydro, however, is not an entirely clean industry and can cause severe environmental damage if mismanaged. In Ireland, the Spirit of Ireland model launched by Irish entrepreneur Graham O'Donnell proposes to combine wind power with hydropower by pumping sea water to high-elevation dams in Ireland's U-shaped gorges to solve the intermittency problem associated with wind and to develop a new source of energy for Ireland.

Nuclear power

Generating a vast amount of energy from a very small quantity of material seems, on the surface, the perfect panacea for depletion in fossil fuels, but, as ever, it's simply not that straightforward. Globally, nuclear power contributes about 6% to overall energy supply. Nuclear power, however, is not evenly spread. In France, nuclear plants generate more than 75% of French electricity. Lithuania is also heavily reliant on nuclear energy from an old Soviet reactor. In the United States, nuclear plants contribute about 20% of US electricity and at the end of 2009 the UK government announced an expansion of its nuclear industry with a further eleven new sites, expecting 40% of British electricity to come from nuclear fission by 2025. Nuclear plants generate electricity by heating water to extremely high temperatures to produce steam to power turbines. Water is heated through nuclear fission, a process in which atoms are split, releasing large amounts of energy.

The Chinese plan to spend $50 billion building thirty-two nuclear plants by 2020. At first glance, this looks like a net increase in world nuclear power. However, a large number of the 435 commercial nuclear reactors operating across thirty countries in 2009 are nearly obsolete, which means that very substantial investment is required simply to maintain the global net output from the nuclear industry. Given the expected increase in electricity demand, the likelihood is that the net contribution from the nuclear industry may decline rather than increase over the years ahead, but investment opportunities remain.

Although the source material, uranium, is very common, only one isotope, uranium 235, is a suitable fuel for the old light-water nuclear reactors, and only 0.7% of the world's uranium is uranium 235. Newer reactors are fuelled by the more abundant uranium 238 and thorium 232 isotopes. When their initial charge is used up, these reactors run on the fuel they have generated themselves, cooling it using liquid metals and recycling the by-product for reuse. In effect, they breed their own fuel, hence the name 'breeder reactor'.

Proponents of the nuclear industry and many classically trained economists believe that nuclear power is the answer to meeting future electricity demand. They argue that the nuclear industry is 'clean' because the level of CO_2 emissions created by the process is zero. This argument is flawed. No weight is given to the impact on the environment from nuclear waste and the substantial CO_2 emissions created by the construction of new nuclear plants. Although the Chinese plan is to build thirty-two nuclear plants by 2020, it is conceivable that China could increase this tenfold by the middle of this century, equalling 70% of the entire global nuclear output today. The race for control of uranium ore is on and prices increased by 1,200% between 2003 and 2007.

Apart from the long lead-time in the construction of new nuclear plants, there is also a limit to the availability of expertise to build and run them, and objections from local and national pressure groups can plague the planning process – where a planning process exists. The lack of nuclear experience shouldn't be underestimated when considering any revival of the global nuclear industry. Finland's new Olkiluoto 3 reactor has been beset by delays and huge cost overruns, a far cry from the on-time and on-budget construction of EDF's latest reactor in France. Nor are nuclear plants as efficient as starry-eyed proponents present: in France, the most efficient nuclear market, the average down time for maintenance and refuelling is 15%. On average, Britain's nuclear plants are not contributing to the grid 50% of the time. The key weakness in the nuclear argument is decommissioning, the cost of which is typically taken off balance sheets and passed on to future generations of taxpayers to absorb. Already, 250,000 tons of toxic nuclear waste have been accumulated by the global nuclear industry and the amount is growing each year with no breakthrough in sight about how to deal with it.

Demand growth for high-grade uranium is increasing at a rate of 3% a year, well ahead of increased output from uranium mines, and it is expected to remain that way for several years. This supply-and-demand tension, which is driving prices higher, isn't helped by the scarcity of suitable ores or the impact of EROEI as it becomes increasingly expensive to extract them. It is likely that these two factors in combination will bring uranium production to a halt around the middle of this century. In a 2006 study by the German Energy Watch Group, world reserves of uranium were predicted to guarantee uranium supply for only thirty more years.

The inevitable depletion of high-grade uranium ore reserves is leading to growth in the reprocessing of spent uranium fuels and plutonium dioxide, in combination with new designs for breeder plants. While this is changing the shape of the nuclear industry, the long lead-time from planning to construction means that the nuclear industry is unlikely to provide the great panacea envisaged by its supporters. Probably the biggest obstacle to nuclear growth is popular resistance to planning applications from pressure groups. But support for the anti-nuclear power lobby may wane significantly if oil and gas supplies become disrupted. Faced with the prospect of having the lights go out and industry grinding to a halt, popular opinion may well be clamouring for the construction of nuclear plants in their back yards. The question then will be whether the change of heart has arrived too late.

The revival of the nuclear industry creates investment opportunities. Opportunities for a pure play on nuclear power suppliers are somewhat restricted – the industry is typically in national ownership – but there are routes into the nuclear-revival trend. ETF Securities has a quoted fund, the **ETFS WNA Global Nuclear**

Energy Fund, listed on the London Stock Market, where its stock-price ticker is, somewhat ironically, **NUKE**. The fund has a spread across the nuclear utilities, construction companies, technology equipment and services, reactors and fuels. Over 60% of uranium supplies are currently coming from mining operators with the remainder coming from reprocessed nuclear fuels and the military.

With a market capitalisation by mid-2009 of $10 billion, the big boy on the block is Toronto-based **Cameco Corporation (NYSE: CCJ)**, a mining group that controls about one-fifth of the market. Cameco has mining operations in Canada and the US and controls approximately 500 million pounds of proven and probable reserves of uranium. In Saskatchewan, where Cameco has its headquarters, it has mining operations where the uranium ore grade is up to 100 times higher than the world average. Cameco owns or controls 40% of the Western world's capacity to produce uranium hexafluoride (UF_6), which is required to produce fuel for light-water reactors. Cameco reckons that 445 million pounds of new uranium production will be required to meet global demand over the next ten years, placing the company in an enviable position.

Cameco is still recovering from a big hit to its share price after the flooding of its core Cigar Lake mine in October 2006, underlining the risks and hazards of mining and of investment in mining shares. Dewatering is underway, however, and if all goes well full production could recommence at Cigar Lake as early as 2012, adding an additional 9 million pounds of uranium to Cameco's annual production. Cigar Lake accounts for about 14% of the net asset value of Cameco, which is projecting a big increase in demand for uranium over the next decade and expects to secure supply agreements with China, where it reckons 2 billion pounds of uranium will eventually be needed.

For a pure play on uranium, but a more speculative or wild card investment, **Uranerz Energy Corporation (AMEX : URZ)** is a small uranium exploration company with uranium properties in Saskatchewan, Mongolia and Wyoming in the USA. Uranerz's core mining asset is in the uranium-rich Powder River Basin in Wyoming, where it owns or controls nearly 180 square miles in the Pumpkin Buttes Uranium Mining District. Since it plans to develop its mining operations further and grow through acquisition, Uranerz may be worth some speculative investment. It is a volatile stock, however, and the timing of any investment will be important.

Hydropower

Hydropower remains the leading source of renewable energy, accounting for 97% of all electricity generated from renewable sources and 20% of global electricity supply. Building hydroelectric plants requires a vast amount of capital and materials, but it is a mature industry that has already captured many of the best locations worldwide for the production of hydropower. Although the sector will not experience the exponential growth now embedded in wind power, solar power, biofuels and other renewable sources, rising electricity costs ramped up by rising oil, gas and coal prices, make investment in hydropower companies attractive.

Water, covering 75% of the earth's surface, became an industrial source of energy with the invention of the waterwheel, which was used to cut stones in ancient Egypt. In the modern world, strongly flowing water is used to generate electricity by powering turbines linked to electricity generators. The top five producers in the world are Canada; the US, where hydropower generates 10% of electricity reaching 28 million residents; the former USSR; Brazil and China, where the Three Gorges Dam will flood an area twice the size of a small country.

Hydropower isn't an entirely clean energy. Building new plants like the Three Gorges consumes vast amounts of materials and energy, emits a great deal of CO_2 and creates environmental and conservation problems. New technologies, such as submerged turbines that turn with river velocity, are playing a part in new designs, but legacy issues remain with older dams. Hydropower's weakness is its seasonality and, for investors, its inability to match the speed of growth in other renewable energy industries like wind and solar. But hydro has the lowest marginal cost for power at about one euro per hundred kilowatt hours, and hydro energy can generate power at times of peak demand by releasing stored water. Hydropower, which is 90% efficient in translating raw energy to electricity, beats fossil fuels at 50%, wind at 30% and photovoltaic solar cells at 12–15%, which is why the Spirit of Ireland model is so interesting. Most quoted utilities have a mix of power sources that includes coal, gas, oil and hydro, but some provide a higher exposure to hydro than others.

Finnish company **Fortum (Helsinki: FUM1V)** provides a play on northern European hydro and nuclear power generation. Fortum, valued at €16 billion in mid-2009, is the leading energy company in much of the Nordic/Baltic Rim region. Fortum generates electricity principally through hydropower, but is also poised to be a major player in the area's nuclear power generation. Fortum was founded in 1998, following the combination of two companies, Imatran Voima and Neste Oyj. Fortum generates nearly 11,000 megawatts (MW) of electricity for Nordic countries, most of which is CO_2 free. Its assets include nuclear power – in 2003, the company committed to invest $186 million in a new nuclear power plant in Finland – combined heat and power plants, wind power and improved hydropower. Fortum also plans extensive investment in wind power generation, which currently accounts for less than 0.5% of its electricity output, with the company having first experimented with wind powered electricity production as early as 1986.

IDACORP Inc. (NYSE: IDA), with a market capitalisation in mid-2009 of $1 billion, is a holding company for Idaho Power Company (IPC), an electricity utility covering 24,000 square miles with franchises in seventy-one cities in Idaho and nine in Oregon. It is a US utility with a high exposure to hydropower, owning and operating seventeen hydroelectric plants and with a 50% share in a further nine through its subsidiary Ida-West. IPC also owns two gas-fired plants, one diesel-powered generator and three coal-fired plants. The group also has interests in real estate.

8. Renewable Energy

Green energy is where the real loot will be made, provided you back a winning technology and business that has secured an adequate supply of finance that will be needed to power these developing companies, some of which are quite small and liable to be blown off course if they are not well managed. The sector will develop all the hallmarks of a gold rush, much like the infamous technology mania of the 1990s. There are going to be lots of losers: busted companies that promise the moon but which eat up all their capital before delivering revenues. But, equally, there will be companies about whom few have yet heard, on track to become household names and that will deliver super long-term returns to early investors, much like Microsoft, Yahoo and Google did from their humble beginnings. However, don't expect beefy companies just yet. The sector contains modest-sized businesses and real minnows and many of the breakthrough companies pioneering green energy are not yet listed and so are unavailable to investors except through private equity firms. Many other valuable green energy initiatives operate as divisions within huge conglomerates with diverse interests and hence don't provide a pure play in this exciting sector.

You can invest in green energy by concentrating on stocks and sectors you select yourself, such as those outlined below, or you can choose a diversified fund to do it for you – but bear in mind that funds will not usually invest in small fast-growing companies until they reach a critical mass, which makes the small-company sector a hunting ground exclusive to investors and private equity funds. Funds also tend not to specialise, providing instead a broad spread across green energy sectors.

There are a number of choices in the fund market with more coming on stream as the sector wins more investor support. The **ETFS DAXglobal Alternative Energy Fund (London: ALTE)** is an ETF with a broad spread of companies across wind, bio-energy, geothermal, natural gas and solar and, much like many ETFs, has a competitive management charge of, in its case, 0.65% per year. Funds also exist in the domestic life-assurance industry, notably Zurich Life's **Green Energy Fund** that combines two ETFs in green energy (75%) and water (25%) and New Ireland's **KBCAM Alternative Energy Fund**, which is actively managed.

Renewable energy enthusiasts have been traditionally regarded as woolly minded environmentalists with an innocent view of how the world works. Times have changed, though. Today we are on the cusp of vast growth in renewable energy of all kinds. Solar, wind and biofuels are becoming huge, with embryonic areas such as geothermal and synthetic fuels growing fast. Remember, the IEA has forecast global expansion in alternative energy over the next two decades at a sizzling 8% per year.

The outlook in this area is rich with possibilities and diversity as the necessary human ingenuity and capital arrive in sufficient quantities to fuel a revolution in renewable energy. Although still accounting for less than 1% of world energy demand, renewable energy is growing at high speed and, when you consider that fossil-fuel emissions and depletion is driving that growth, its exponential nature is guaranteed.

Climate change

Climate change is the key driver behind the growth in the renewable energy sector, and it's not going away. Peak oil and rising prices will become irrelevant if the planet becomes uninhabitable. Scientific evidence that CO_2 emissions are responsible for potentially catastrophic climate change is now largely accepted worldwide and renewable energy is part of the solution. Policy makers throughout the world, but especially in the European Union, have set market share targets and created incentives for the growth of renewable energy. Countries concerned about the security of their energy supply know that building up domestic renewable energy resources lessens the threat to their economies. Increased investment and breakthroughs in technology are improving renewable energy efficiency and the previously high break-even hurdles are falling as oil prices rise. The early signs of investment returns, uncorrelated to general equities, are already there – over 2006 and 2007 investment in the broader renewable energy sector outperformed equity markets by 150% to 200% before the bust.

Quite apart from the economics, there is the overarching and more serious issue of environmental degradation. Fossil and nuclear fuels deplete the earth's natural resources and create radiation, air pollution and acid rain. The emissions of greenhouse gases from fossil-fuel combustion pose an enormous threat to humanity.

The greenhouse effect is a natural process which keeps the earth at a temperate average of 15°C as the presence of gases in the atmosphere, including carbon dioxide, water vapour, nitrous oxide and methane, act much like a greenhouse, keeping heat radiated from the earth's surface from escaping entirely into space. Shorn of the greenhouse effect, the earth's average temperature would be a chilly −18°C, but the increase in greenhouse gases resulting from the accelerated industrialisation of the global economy throughout the course of the twentieth century means that the average temperature of the world is rising. The concentration of carbon dioxide in the atmosphere has increased by over a third from the pre-industrialisation levels of the mid-1700s and is now higher than its estimated previous peak 650,000 years ago. CO_2 emissions increased by 70% between 1970 and 2004.

Predicting the effects of climate change is a tricky business, but polar ice-cap melting is already evident, as is plant and animal migration, the spread of malaria to higher latitudes and an increase in severe weather events such as storms and droughts. The UN Intergovernmental Panel on Climate Change (UNIPCC), established in 1988, has produced four conclusive reports on the effect that humans are having on climate change.

To limit global warming to between 2°C and 2.4°C above pre-industrial levels, carbon dioxide emissions will have to peak shortly and then reduce to between 50% and 85% of their levels in 2000. Average world economic growth is expected to be around 2.5% a year, ignoring the impact of climate change on growth. But, the cost of climate change of 2°C is calculated to reduce world GDP by between 1% and 2%. An average increase in temperatures of 3.5°C is expected to reduce GDP by 5%. Consequently, tackling climate change is critical to avoid a prolonged worldwide recession.

The IPCC model estimates that if the worst effects of climate change peak as quickly as 2015, a reduction in global GDP of just 0.12% by 2030 could be possible. A critical weapon in the armoury is charging for carbon emissions to influence how fossil fuels are used in the future. The cost of carbon emissions will increase exponentially over the years, fuelling strong growth in emissions trading.

In October 2006 Nicholas Stern, the British former chief economist of the World Bank, released his seminal *Stern Review on the Economics of Climate Change*. Stern stated bluntly that the economic damage created by global warming is likely to be between 5% and 20% per year of global GDP if no action is taken. He calculated that, to avoid the worst effects of climate change, 1% of GDP would need to be invested in carbon-free energy, energy efficiency, emissions reduction and trading, and education.

Economists criticising the Stern report say that Stern used the most pessimistic assumptions and magnified the impact in the distant future to rationalise major cuts in CO_2 emissions today. Others plainly reject the science that human activity and CO_2 emissions are causing the climate to warm and believe it to be a natural process that human actions cannot influence. But the reality is that climate change has been accepted throughout the world as being caused by man-made CO_2 emissions and that urgent policy change is required.

The Kyoto Protocol

The 1997 Kyoto Protocol to the United Nations Framework Convention on Climate Change (UNFCCC) was signed by 174 countries, though not the USA, and contains legally binding emission targets for developed countries based on 1990 levels. The targeted reduction in each signatory's emissions must be achieved within the period 2008 to 2012. Signatories have agreed to reduce their collective emissions of six greenhouse gases by at least 5%, with the EU committed to 8% cuts. But, owing to continually rising emissions, the actual reduction targets will be larger than 5% and are more likely to be in the region of 20% by 2010. By the end of 2009, 189 countries had ratified the Kyoto Protocol, but they did not include the US. China and India have ratified the Protocol but are not required to reduce CO_2 emissions. Countries are given flexibility on how they meet reductions, for example by purchasing so-called carbon credits.

An international emissions trading regime has been established to enable industrialised countries to trade emission credits between themselves. The Kyoto Protocol, which envisages higher emissions-cutting targets for those who don't comply, can suspend member countries from involvement in the emissions-trading programme if necessary. It is highly likely that carbon-credits will become the world's most-traded commodity as exchanges are established, transparency is implemented, prices are set and industrial entities begin to buy and sell them.

The EU has been leading the field in renewable energy targets and in CO_2 emissions. The EU fines members for failing to meet their obligations under Kyoto and established an emissions trading scheme in December 2002. The fines, which started at €40 per ton of CO_2 in 2005, had already risen to €100 per ton by 2008. The successor to the Kyoto Protocol was finalised in December 2007 in Bali, the foundation for which was laid by the G8 leaders (including the United States), who met earlier that year in Germany, pledging to reduce greenhouse gases by at least 50% by 2050.

Bali

Meeting in Bali in December 2007, 190 parties to the UNFCCC bound developed countries, including the US, to agree to greenhouse gas emission reduction targets. The Bali agreement was really a road map for the 2009 talks in Copenhagen and set up a process by which a series of steps and targets could be mutually agreed referencing the UN IPCC latest recommendation for a 25% to 40%

reduction by 2020. One of the key breakthroughs at Bali was the inclusion of emissions from deforestation and forest degradation in developing countries.

Copenhagen

In December 2009 world leaders struck a new political accord which set out explicit emission pledges and that included China for the first time. The UN Climate Change Conference in Copenhagen, however, after two weeks of disagreement and in a last-minute deal brokered by US president Barack Obama, did not set legally binding targets, postponing this thorny issue until either the next meeting in Mexico in 2010 or in South Africa the following year. Instead an aspirational objective to limit global temperatures rises to 2°C by mid-century was set, together with a collective promise from developed countries to contribute $30 billion per annum until 2012 to help developing countries reduce emissions, preserve forests and prepare for climate change. The intention is to increase this to $100 billion annually by 2020. The game moves on to Mexico in late November 2010, where attempts will be made to progress from a political accord to a legally binding one and to resolve the opposing economic interests of the two main emitters, China and the USA.

Europe takes the lead

The EU has led the way in greenhouse gas and energy policy. It's easy to understand why – the EU currently imports 57% of its gas and 82% of its oil. The EU policy objective is to create a low-carbon economy, improve security of supply and increase competition in energy markets. The primary targets are:

To achieve a 20% cut in CO_2 emissions (compared to 1990 levels) by 2020 (or 30% if agreed by the Bali process).

To meet 20% of all energy demand from renewable sources by 2020.

To cut CO_2 emissions by 50% by 2050.

To implement 10% of biofuels in the fuel mix by 2020.

To increase energy efficient savings by 20% of all EU energy by 2020.

To implement a technology plan aimed at developing technologies and renewable energy, low-energy buildings, clean coal and carbon-capture technologies and to build next-generation nuclear power.

To create a link to Africa to develop the continent as a sustainable energy supplier to the EU.

Individual countries, such as Ireland and the UK, are reacting with their own targets. In Ireland, a renewable electricity target of 15% has been set for 2010, up from 8.5% in 2006. One-third of electricity consumption by 2020 must come from renewable sources and an east–west electricity interconnector is to be built by 2012. In the UK, 15% of energy must come from renewable sources by 2015 compared to 5% in 2007. The UK government is placing a heavy emphasis on wind through tax incentives. All new homes are to be carbon-neutral buildings by no later than 2016.

Security is the other driver of energy supply, not just the physical delivery of energy, which is open to political risk, but also the relative impact of accelerating prices for fossil fuels. Ireland is particularly exposed, being 93% dependent on imported fossil fuels.

New technologies

On the other side of the coin, technological advances are significantly reducing costs. In the solar market, technological improvements in creating thinner wafers mean that less silicon is needed per solar cell and therefore costs are lower. Average thickness of wafers has been reduced by nearly 50% from 0.32mm in 2003 to 0.18mm in 2007 and further improvements in efficiency of up to 17.5% are expected over the next two years.

On the wind energy side, the increase in turbine size from less than 1MW in the 1980s to up to 5MW today has reduced fixed costs and increased efficiency. However, with the advent of rising oil prices, more money is now being invested in breakthrough technologies across the whole ambit of renewable energy, as well as improving the efficiency of existing energy sources. Economic growth goes hand in hand with growth in energy supply as one cannot happen without the other. The International Energy Agency forecasts growth in global primary demand of 55% by 2030 with electricity demand projected to double, based on an annual growth rate of 2.8% a year. CO_2 emissions from power plants are expected to increase by at least two-thirds over this period with China and India contributing 60% of the rise.

Wind energy

Wind energy has been with us for a long time. At least as early as 200 BC, the Chinese were using wind energy to pump water while, in the Middle East, wind power was used to grind grain. In modern times, windmills re-emerged to generate electricity as early as 1890 in Denmark. When the wind blows, the sails on a windmill, which are attached to a rotor linked to a generator, create electrical current. Breakthroughs in wind turbine technology have increased the electricity efficiency per kilowatt to the same level as fossil fuels; however, the development of wind turbines itself has been affected by rising commodity prices, especially for steel. Europe is leading the rest of the world in the development of wind energy, but there is also rapid expansion in the United States.

In 2006 alone the total value of the new wind energy plants installed was €18 billion, with wind installations in over seventy countries and year-on-year growth reckoned to be in excess of 30%. In Europe, the highest installed wind capacity is in Germany, followed by Spain and Denmark. Globally, the US, India and new players like China and France are catching up. Total installed wind capacity worldwide is reckoned to be about 75,000MW, approximately 1.5% of global electricity demand.

Total installations are forecast to increase wind output globally to 150,000MW by 2010. Europe is expected to continue to contribute strongly, adding an average of 9,000MW per year to reach a total of 130,000MW by 2015. This is from a base of 48,000MW at the end of 2006. In the US and before the acceleration created by Obama's stimulus, wind power was expected to increase from 11,000MW in 2006 to nearly 50,000MW in 2015, with more than $65 billion forecast to be invested in additional wind capacity by 2015. Offshore wind capacity is expected to grow very strongly from a small base as planning processes ease, incentives kick in and technical challenges are solved.

Wind turbines have a typical tower height of between 60 and 80 metres with blades between 30 and 40 metres long. Individual turbines generate between 1.5 and 5MW with offshore wind turbines producing at the higher end of the scale but requiring protection from salt corrosion. The lifetime of a wind turbine is normally estimated at twenty years and costs per turbine range from over €1 million for an onshore turbine to close to €2 million for an offshore turbine.

Tall wind turbines allow greater capture of wind at higher speed and less turbulent currents. But, despite this fact, wind is variable and can produce viable electricity only when blowing strongly enough and in the right direction. Stanford University undertook a study in 2000 looking at some of the world's windiest areas, including northern Europe, the North Sea, Tasmania, the Great Lakes and the northeastern and northwestern coasts of North and South America. The study concluded that wind could potentially generate sufficient electrical power to satisfy world electricity needs sevenfold.

So growth in wind energy will continue to be substantial and, over time, it is likely to replace nuclear energy in terms of its efficiency per kilowatt hour provided its Achilles heel, intermittent supply, can be cured by technological developments in systems of storage and distribution.

INVESTING IN WIND ENERGY

With a market capitalisation in mid-2009 at €10 billion, **Vestas Wind Systems (Copenhagen: VWS)** is one of the largest suppliers of wind turbines in the world and operates over 35,000 of them across sixty-three countries. The profitability of Vestas Wind Systems may be tested by increased competition in this sector and changes in technology; however, it still remains the biggest player on the block.

Vestas' story is one of astounding success, having installed its first wind turbine in 1979 and moving from sixty employees in 1987 to over 15,000, twenty years later. Vestas is estimated to have 23% of world market share and claims it establishes an average of one wind turbine every four hours. Worldwide, its operational turbines are estimated to generate more than 16 million megawatt hours of electricity each year.

Spanish company **Gamesa S.A. (Madrid: GAM)**, with a market capitalisation in mid-2009 of €4 billion, is the second largest wind turbine manufacturer in the world and has divested itself of its solar assets to focus purely on wind turbine manufacturing and wind farm development. Its international sales account for 62% of its revenues and its profits have exceeded most analysts' forecasts. Gamesa continues to display strong growth and is a contender for any investment in wind.

Having aggressively expanded into the United States, another Spanish company, **Iberdrola (Madrid: IBE)**, is now operating in over twenty countries. Iberdrola reached a total installed capacity of over 8,000MW in the first quarter of 2008, consolidating its position as a leader in world wind power. Its plan is to increase its capacity by 2,000MW on an annual basis, aiming to reach 13,600MW by 2010.

Clipper Wind Power PLC (London: CWP), valued by the markets at £185 million, is another fast-growing company engaged in wind energy technology, turbine manufacture and project development. With offices in the US, Mexico, Denmark and the UK, Clipper Wind Power manufactures and assembles wind turbines from a plant in Iowa. As the wind industry consolidates, and larger players move into it, it is likely that smaller players like Clipper Wind Power could become a takeover target.

CHINESE AND INDIAN WIND

Since 2005 China has made enormous strides to promote renewable energy. In 2007 the Chinese government announced plans to underpin growth in renewable energy to reach 10% of total energy consumption by 2010 and 15% by 2020. This includes a stipulation that electricity suppliers must purchase a certain amount of electricity generated from renewable sources. Tariff incentives are being provided for renewable energy production and the higher costs will be borne by purchasers and users. Subsidies and preferential tax treatment are being provided for renewable energy projects. The Chinese government has set targets for 2020 of 300 gigawatts (GW) of hydroelectric power, 30GW in wind generation, 30GW from biomass and 1.8GW from solar energy. To fund this growth the Chinese government will need to invest $270 billion by 2020 in renewable energy.

Wind energy has caught on in India where **Suzlon Energy (Mumbai: SUZL)**, with a market capitalisation of €2 billion, dominates the local market. Suzlon is in the process of building Asia's largest wind park, in Dhule, Maharshta, which will have a capacity of over 1,000MW when completed. Suzlon is ranked the fifth largest wind turbine supplier in the world with over 10.5% of market share in 2007. It employs over 13,000 people with operations in twenty countries, including the United States and Europe. Much like Vestas Wind Systems, the Suzlon story is one of spectacular growth, having been established in 1995 with just twenty employees by Tulsi Tanti, a textile manufacturer who, faced with frequent interruptions in the supply of electricity, looked to wind to power his business. In 2006 Suzlon acquired Hansen Transmissions of Belgium, the second largest gearbox manufacturer in the world, and has sought growth outside India in the United States, Brazil, China, Italy and Portugal. Suzlon offers a range of turbines varying in capacity from 350kW to 2.1MW and for a variety of climates.

Although not a pure wind energy player, **China Hi-Speed Transmission (Hong Kong/Frankfurt: 0658)** manufactures wind turbines and is the dominant player in China, accounting for 90% of wind turbine gearboxes. Nearly a third of the company's revenues came from the wind energy sector and represents the company's fastest growing business. China's 70% local-content rule for wind turbines means that manufacturers in Chinese markets have to use local component suppliers for their turbines.

CARBON FIBRE CHALLENGING STEEL

One of the biggest problems facing wind turbine manufacturers is the availability of steel, which has been subject to rapidly escalating prices as the commodity bull market continues. This is what makes **Zoltec Companies Inc. (NASDAQ: ZOLT)** interesting. With a market capitalisation of $315 million by mid-2009, Zoltec manufactures carbon fibres used as the primary building material in commercial products, including wind turbines. Zoltec plans to lead the commercialisation of carbon fibre as the primary composite building material having entered the carbon fibre business through an acquisition in 1988 that gave Zoltec access to technology for new high-capacity aircraft brakes and for the supply of carbon fibre for rocket nozzles at NASA. Zoltec took the technology designed for aerospace carbon fibres and looked at ways of reducing the costs and price of this exceptionally strong, yet lightweight, material, which was central to its initial public offering (IPO) in 1992. Zoltec's annual sales growth target is ambitious – $500 million by 2011, which would be a 500% increase on its sales revenue for 2007 – and targeting, in particular, wind energy, alternative energy, fuel-efficient cars, construction and infrastructure, and oil exploration.

Solar energy

No wonder we marvel at the winter solstice at Newgrange, how the first shaft of morning light is perfectly aligned to brighten the inner chamber – we've become so used to electricity it's easy to forget that without the sun there would be no life on earth, which is why the sun was deified by pagan religions throughout the world and was the centrepiece of the ancient Egyptian culture. The sun is the origin of all energy, including fossil fuels, and sun strikes the earth every minute with solar energy in excess of the total amount of fossil fuels the planet burns in a year.

Photovoltaic (PV) cells translate the energy created by sunlight into electricity. Japan is the market leader at 37% of PV cell production, followed by Germany at 20% and China at 15%. The total installed PV generation capacity globally has increased from approximately 1,500MW just nine years ago to in excess of 8,000MW today and is growing at an annual compound rate of 30%. While the PV industry in Europe, the US, China and Japan is investing heavily in new facilities, the political directives for the development of solar electricity are moving at pace in the US, Germany and Spain in particular.

The development of electricity from PV cells has traditionally been very expensive, with high operating costs compared to conventional fossil-fuel sources. This equation, however, is changing as oil prices rise and PV expands in areas with high solar energy and strong subsidies, such as California. Compared to the wholesale electricity market, PV power is expensive and is expected to remain so for some years to come. Developments, however, which enable rooftop-based PV systems to feed directly into the grid in Germany, Japan and the United States, where PV electricity costs about the same as retail electricity, is creating a growing market.

The advantage of solar energy is that the sun provides the fuel and there are no moving parts and minimal maintenance. Solar energy is silent and there are no harmful emissions. The problem with solar energy is its EROEI. The production of PV cells requires a large amount of electricity and the payback period can be between two and five years. The strength of sunlight at many locations is also an issue and, based on current technology, energy conversion is still low. Obviously there is no power at night, and it is impaired by overcast conditions.

Although solar energy has been used for heating for many centuries, it wasn't until 1955 that the first patented silicon-based solar cell emerged.

PV technology is used to generate power by converting light into electricity using solar cells, mostly made from crystalline silicon wafers. Another category of cells, thin-film solar cells, don't use silicon but are made by coating photosensitive materials on glass or steel. A third method, solar thermal energy, uses the strength of the sun directly for immediate heating or to heat fluids to create steam to drive turbines.

The main growth in the market will be in PV cells and the technological direction is likely to be in thin-film solar cells, which, because no silicon is used, can be mass-produced for a fraction of the cost. This puts China into play as it is likely to become the dominant producer in the solar industry over the years ahead, given its capacity to manufacture electronics more quickly and more cheaply than many more developed countries. More efficiency and lower production costs, coupled with policy-driven incentives, are creating strong year-on-year growth for solar energy.

Technology is improving the efficiency with which the heat absorbed by solar cells is converted to power, reducing the amount of energy lost in the process. Already, over a ten-year period, the efficiency of solar cells has increased 100% and earlier experimentation indicates the potential to double it again.

INVESTING IN SOLAR ENERGY

There are several avenues into the solar energy market, from investing in large manufacturers of PV cells to cutting-edge innovators in flexible solar tiles designed to change the way we use rooftops to generate energy. It's a fast-growing, diverse and exciting market.

With a market capitalisation in mid-2009 of $14 billion, **Applied Materials (NASDAQ: AMAT)** is the largest producer of chip-making equipment in the world. It stands to benefit from the growth of the solar industry and is a leader in nano-manufacturing technologies, specialising in the fabrication of semi-conductor chips, solar PV cells and other types of electronics. Founded in 1967, Applied Materials, with headquarters in Santa Clara in the United States, has a diversified revenue stream, dominated by silicon, accounting for about 60% of sales, and with good exposure towards fast-developing markets of South East Asia, Korea and Taiwan. Applied Materials employs 14,500 people worldwide and its net sales in 2007 were $9.73 billion.

LDK Solar (NYSE: LDK), whose IPO was in June 2007, is the leading Chinese manufacturer of multi-crystalline solar ingots and wafers and had a market capitalisation of $1 billion in mid-2009. Its production capacity is expected to grow strongly from sales of solar wafers between 180 and 220 microns in thickness. LDK is constructing a polysilicon plant in Xinyu city in the province of Jiangxi with a capacity, in 2008, of up to 6,000 metric tons and 15,000 metric tons by the end of 2009.

Energy Conversion Devices (NASDAQ: ENER) manufactures thin-film solar laminates converting sunlight into energy using proprietary technology. Its products are aimed at roofing applications and are designed to be lightweight, durable and flexible enough to be easily integrated with building materials to generate more energy. ECD is regarded as the leader in thin-film technology in the solar industry and was valued by the market by mid-2009 at $735 million. It is a differentiated solar company positioned in the middle of a fast-growing niche sector.

Based in Vancouver, British Columbia, **Xantrex Technology Inc. (Toronto: XTX)**, valued by the market by mid-2009 at CAD48 million (about $30 million), is a small specialist company that manufactures a product designed to convert raw electrical power, generated at power plants, back into the grid. Its series of inverter/charges convert raw direct current (DC) generated at power plants back into alternating current (AC). This places its conversion solution as a renewable energy and a back-up for power applications. Xantrex converters also convert DC power from battery storage into reliable AC electricity for use in the home or business, making it useful in areas which have an intermittent or unreliable electricity supply. Xantrex employs approximately 830 people and had revenues in 2007 of CAD234 million.

Bio-energy

Bio-energy is just a fancy name for some of our oldest sources of energy and is derived from organic matter. This includes energy crops, as well as trees, agricultural food, waste, feed crops, wood waste, animal waste, etc., called the feedstock. There are two main processes. The most common is combustion, which involves burning the feedstock to produce steam to drive turbines to create electricity. The second process, anaerobic digestion, creates gas which is used to fuel gas engines or burned in a boiler to produce steam or heat. In liquid form, bio-energy is known as biofuel and is increasingly used throughout the world for transportation. Biofuel is generated from sugar, vegetable oil, animal fats and starch and is produced as either ethanol or esters (biodiesel). Ethanol is mostly produced from sugar and starchy crops and is blended with petrol. Biodiesel, on the other hand, is mainly produced from soya beans and oilseed crops such as rape and sunflowers.

In the early days of the automotive industry, the combustion engine was designed to run on ethanol and the diesel engine to run on peanut oil. Technology improvements and rising oil prices are driving interest in biofuels, but with the exception of Brazil, which is the only country in the world where biofuels compete on price with conventional petrol and diesel, the cost of producing biofuels has acted as a disincentive. This is now changing dramatically. In 2005 global production of biofuels amounted to approximately 400,000 barrels per day, sufficient to meet 1% of road transport fuel demand. Brazil, responding to the 1973 oil crisis, set a target to drastically reduce its imported oil bill over twenty years. In doing so, it created the largest ethanol market in the world and a giant company, Petrobras. Brazilian ethanol producers became competitive against petrol when crude-oil prices rose above $40 dollars a barrel.

The second largest producer of ethanol in the world is the United States. The IEA estimates annual biofuel growth at 7% per year to 2030, by which time biofuels could meet 3% of world transport fuel demands. But the potential for biofuels could be higher as policies drive the market and technological breakthroughs increase the space for it.

Ethanol dominates this sector, taking 86% of the biofuel market, with biodiesel accounting for the remaining 14%. Ethanol is produced by the fermentation of sugars by enzymes and can be made from just about anything that can be converted into sugar. Sugar cane and sugar beet contain sugar which is then fermented and distilled. Corn, barley and wheat contain starch that can be changed into sugar and then into ethanol.

Biodiesel is typically made from soya bean oil, rape or sunflower seed oil, palm oil and animal fat through a process called transesterification, which generates fatty-acid methyl esters.

DO FUEL CROPS DESERVE A BAD PRESS?

Much has been made about the tension between fuel crops and food crops and that the growing of biofuels, especially ethanol, is leading to food price inflation. But there are good biofuels and bad biofuels. In the United States, most ethanol is made from corn and, in 2007, US farmers grew over 13 billion bushels of corn on 85 million acres, of which a little over 20% went to make 7 billion gallons of ethanol. But that still left enough to satisfy both the US market and a record demand for exports. If US farmers can continue to produce corn-based ethanol without impacting on food output, the same could hold true in many European countries, including Ireland, for the production of other types of biofuel crops on non-food-producing lands. Damage to the environment and direct competition with food crops, however, is occurring elsewhere in the developing world as deforestation makes more arable land and existing food crops are replaced by more profitable biofuel feedstock. Food price inflation can be impacted by other factors, including a sharp increase in global demand, rising oil and gas prices and climate factors such as the recent drought in Australia and floods in Argentina, two large wheat producers.

Producing ethanol from corn, however, is not as efficient as producing it from Brazilian sugar cane, which is why companies worldwide are beating a path to Brazilian partners to make biodiesel, biogasoline and jet fuel from sugar cane and why Brazil is now a net exporter of bio-ethanol. Biofuel can also be made from feedstocks that don't compete with food supplies, displace crops or cause CO_2 emissions from forest destruction, such as switch grass, which has 9ft deep roots and thrives in arid regions.

Biodiesel, made from the process of transesterification and then mixed with alcohol to convert it into a fuel, is 100% biodegradable and both safer and cleaner than petroleum diesel. Although soya bean oil is currently the most economical source for biodiesel, it can also be made from rape seed, mustard, palm oil, canola oil and algae. Biodiesel can be used 100% as a fuel in engines or can be blended with regular diesel. The IEA estimates that in the United States alone, biodiesel production is set to grow to 400 million gallons by 2030. In Europe, driven by directives, biodiesel will also contribute significantly to the European renewable energy targets.

The cutting edge in the advances in the production of biodiesel is in producing it from certain types of algae rather than from feedstock. These simple water-based organisms capture light and create a type of vegetable oil. Algae can be grown anywhere with sunlight but the process still requires high amounts of energy, which is why innovators in algae biodiesel are positioning their plants adjacent to existing power plants to benefit from the surplus heat they create.

Biofuels, of course, are not a panacea. There simply isn't enough suitable unused arable land and water to grow sufficient feedstock to meet global biofuel demand, particularly for transportation, and even with currently high and rising oil prices the EROEI is unattractive. Nevertheless, the market for biofuels as part of the energy mix is set to grow exponentially, but challenges remain. Policies will need to be carefully balanced to ensure that a large-scale switch to growing biofuel feedstocks does not lead to deforestation, loss of animal habitat, increased poverty and hegemony by big international corporations squeezing small family farmers.

Unquestionably there will be winners and losers in the biofuel sector as oil prices rise. The losers will be feedstock consumers in the agriculture sector who will face higher costs for cattle feed. US ethanol, made from a large chunk of the annual US corn crop, is dependent on energy prices. First, there is the gas used to manufacture the vast amounts of fertiliser needed to support the crop.

Second, embedded in the harvesting process, is the oil required to fuel large-scale agricultural plant. Finally, there is the coal burned to generate the electricity used in the distillation process. Arguably corn-derived ethanol wouldn't exist at all if it weren't for the subsidies and supports underpinning the market.

INVESTING IN BIOFUELS

One clear way to invest in biofuels is to buy shares in Brazilian giant **Petrobras (NYSE: PBR)**, which controls the lion's share of the ethanol market. For more on Petrobras, see page 107.

Biodiesel production is still in its infancy. Companies are small and young, but with plenty of upside and also plenty of risk, very high risk. Parts of the sector are under strain as feedstock prices escalate in line with increasing commodity prices. There are a number of investment opportunities available through the over-the-counter (OTC) market, off main stock exchanges in penny stocks, tiny companies with huge potential but also the risk of implosion – something not for the fainthearted.

Valcent Products Inc. (OTC and Munich/Berlin: VCTPF) is a minnow but a pioneer in eco-technology aiming to grow agricultural products intensely. With headquarters in Vancouver, British Columbia, Valcent is a penny share trading in mid-2009 at 6 cents a share and is a highly leveraged company. Valcent owns 50% of Vertigro, which has developed an algae production technology for Valcent feedstocks. Valcent has developed a bio-reactor for growing algae to yield high-grade vegetable oils, which can be converted into biodiesel. In addition to its use in this sector, Valcent's high-density vegetable-growing system has been operating in the production of leafy lettuce, micro-green spinach herbs, mixed beets, strawberry sweet grass, alfalfa and other grains, promising to produce vegetables twenty times more efficiently than those grown in a field while requiring only 5% of the water used for field crops. Valcent's Algae Vertical bio-reactor promises an algae biomass production of 276 tons of algae per acre per year. The Algae Vertical bio-reactor technology is being developed jointly with another company, Global Green Solutions Inc., with both companies owning 50% and subject to a 4.5% royalty.

GreenShift Corporation (OTC and Frankfurt: GERS) is a tiny company, trading in mid-2009 at just 1 cent a share. GreenShift has a patented bio-reactor process for growing algae in the exhaust gas streams of fossil-fuel power plants. It also has technologies involved in the extraction of crude vegetable oil from a co-production of corn/ethanol and others aimed at enhancing the chemical conversion of fats and oils into biodiesel. GreenShift is a purely speculative play in the embryonic algae biofuel market.

Geothermal energy

Geothermal energy, which is produced by the internal heat of the earth, is a wonderfully clean, emission-free source of power that is renewable, so long as the rate of heat extraction does not exceed the rate at which the thermal reservoir is renewed by heat from the earth's magma. Typically, geothermal reservoirs that tap into the earth's heat have a life span of between thirty and fifty years before the plant's equipment wears out, although the world's first geothermal plant in Larderello, Italy, was commissioned in 1913 and is still producing!

Geothermal power is conventionally acquired by drilling to depths of between 5,000 and 10,000 feet in locations above cracks in the earth's crust to tap into steam, which is then used to drive turbines to generate electricity. More modern binary plants have a heat exchanger that uses special fluids rather than steam to transfer the energy from the geothermal spring to the turbines. In Iceland, utility companies hope to drill 2.5 miles into the earth's crust in order to tap into steam superheated by magma to temperatures of nearly 482°C. There are many other spots throughout the world which have high geothermal potential, including Hawaii and other parts of the Pacific region.

But, despite its attractiveness, the geothermal market is still embryonic. Setting up a geothermal plant has always been a high-risk business, expensive to set up and with no guarantee of success. Improvements in technology may reduce these risks, however, and the benefits are obvious. Geothermal generators produce zero emissions and have a small carbon footprint. Once up and running they are self-powered and typically run at over 95% capacity from an all but inexhaustible geothermal energy supply. Although the United States is currently the largest market for geothermal power, it is now being used as a source of electricity in Russia, Indonesia, New Zealand, Mexico, Italy and Japan. Both Iceland and the Philippines use geothermal energy to supply 20% of their national electricity needs.

INVESTING IN GEOTHERMAL ENERGY

Some of the companies available for investment tend to be small, but have substantial upside potential. Unlike the hydro market, which, in most developed countries, is fairly mature and where most of the best natural locations are already in use, the geothermal market is still virgin. Nevertheless, some chunky players already exist and others are in early stage, hoovering up leases on locations with high geothermal potential.

Ormat Technologies (NYSE: ORA) is one of the largest and was valued by the market in mid-2009 at $1.7 billion. Ormat is an established player in the US geothermal market and describes itself as a vertically integrated company whose primary business is to develop, own and operate geothermal and recoverable energy regeneration power plants, utilising in-house designed and manufactured equipment. It also supplies other operators with geothermal and recoverable energy regeneration equipment of its own design and manufacture. By the end of the first quarter of 2008, Ormat had seven geothermal plants in the United States, two in Guatemala and one each in Kenya and Nicaragua. Based in Reno, Nevada, Ormat is the third largest geothermal power producer in the US, having built or supplied 1,000MW of geothermal capacity, owning 410MW and holding seventy-five US patents for its proprietary technologies with another thirteen pending.

Two other companies quoted in the US markets are acquiring leases in locations with geothermal potential across the United States. During the Carter administration in the late 1970s, the US Department of Energy was given an instruction to develop a new non-petroleum source of domestic energy. Raft River, Idaho, was identified as a location for research because, as early as the end of the nineteenth century, local ranchers had discovered hot geothermal water while drilling irrigation wells. **US Geothermal (AMEX: HTM)**, with a market capitalisation in mid-2009 of $80 million, has a right to acquire the Raft River geothermal project, but is not yet generating revenues from geothermal energy.

The second company is **Raser Technologies Inc. (NYSE: RZ)**, with a market capitalisation in mid-2009 of $260 million. It operates a twin-approach strategy with one side of its business concentrating on acquiring geothermal leases and the other involved in developing a patented Symetron electromagnetic motor system designed for use in hybrid cars, promising a breakthrough in electric motor technology. Whether a motor car is a hybrid-electric, battery-electric or uses hydrogen fuel cells, they each rely on an electric motor to drive the vehicle. Raser hopes that its innovation will help remove some of the biggest barriers to the widespread use of electric vehicles.

9. Energy Efficiency

Investing in businesses that are at important crossroads in energy production sectors throughout the world makes lots of sense. But, remember, as oil and gas prices rise, there will be an explosion in new products and services designed to do all kinds of jobs using less energy. Those companies providing the most energy-efficient solutions will become market leaders. Lots of existing products, like gas-guzzling SUVs and patio heaters, will become obsolete or face substitution. No matter where you look, there are market leaders who simply didn't take the energy story seriously enough and others who did and who've already invested heavily and are ahead of the game. These will be the winners as we enter the Age of Scarcity. They will eat up their competitors' market share as consumers and businesses become ultra-sensitive to energy costs. The potential areas of investment are growing at speed: as new inventions and improvements in efficiency emerge, existing markets are disrupted and investment opportunities created.

With most newly arriving investors preoccupied with commodities and energy production, the timing is good to invest in energy efficiency, a vast but often overlooked area that includes insulation, fuel efficiency, more effective lighting systems, greater energy efficiency in general in all kinds of applications and industrial processes. This means looking for value across huge industries, such as the motor industry, capital goods, semiconductors and construction, picking companies who are possible winners already ahead of the posse in the energy-efficiency game and who are also responding to climate change, another main driver of the future.

At the end of 2007, following the UN climate change conference in Bali, a raft of environmentally friendly announcements were made by several countries, including the US, France, Ireland, Spain and Germany. The French propose to penalise cars emitting more than 160g of CO_2 per kilometre. Ireland announced its first carbon budget, which banned traditional lightbulbs in favour of energy-saving alternatives from 2009 and penalised high-emission vehicles from July 2008. The Spanish government announced it would hand out €1 billion in direct subsidies to renovate old, energy-inefficient homes and offered another €2 billion yearly in credit to help make homes become between 35% and 60% more energy efficient. In Germany, fourteen separate pieces of legislation were passed to reduce greenhouse gas emissions by 2020. The US announced proposals to raise automobile fuel-economy standards for the first time in three decades to 35 miles per gallon by 2020.

Companies specialising in energy efficiency

The race is on for energy efficiency and the place to look is across automobiles, capital goods, semiconductors and building materials, as well as in specialist sectors like smart metering, fuel cells and even railways! In the fundamental shift now underway, assets and companies that are poorly positioned, those negatively exposed to high energy-led inflation, will suffer greatly. We know this from what happened in the 1970s. Investors will downgrade the price they are prepared to pay for undifferentiated or general-type companies not in the game. P/E ratios are likely to fall into single digits once again for companies that are experiencing high energy-led input costs but are not benefiting from energy-led sales. For this reason, it is vital that equity portfolios, whether held directly or through fund managers, are filtered to examine their bias, negatively or positively, towards the energy story. Companies with high negative exposure should be shed.

It's just a question of time before ETFs will be developed to give investors pure plays on energy efficiency. An independent US research firm, CRB Research LLC, has developed an index, comprising thirty-six companies – North American (59%), European (33%) and Asian (8%) – that is expected to develop into an ETF. The **CRB Energy Efficiency Index (KWHX)** covers companies as small as €250 million in market capitalisation but also covers larger companies.

You can grow your money by investing in businesses that are positively biased towards energy-efficiency gains. The trick is to look for market leaders in each segment, strong companies enjoying a dominant position which is likely to continue into the future, and to mix these with some speculative plays in smaller companies that have the potential to double or treble the value of an investment over time.

Let's start with a basic insulation company. **Rockwool International AS (Copenhagen: ROCKB)**, with a market capitalisation of €1.2 billion in mid-2009, is the world's largest manufacturer of insulation mineral fibres. Rockwool has been around for a long time; it was founded in 1909 and employs 8,500 workers operating from twenty-three plants. During the 1970s oil crisis, Rockwool's revenues from sales, principally in Scandinavia and Germany, jumped 450%. Rockwool's product saves 100 times more energy than is used in its manufacture, according to the company, and it reduces CO_2 emissions because it reduces the need to burn fossil fuels. In addition to its insulation qualities, it doubles as a fire-resistant barrier and is able to withstand heat of more than 1,000°C. Rockwool is a pure play on energy efficiency since 90% of group sales are in insulation products and it generates most of its sales from Germany, which accounts for 15% of its revenues. About 80% of Rockwool's sales come from within Europe, with Eastern Europe now taking up 22%. In 1995, Rockwool moved from being a family-owned business to a public company by floating on the Copenhagen Stock Exchange and, in 2000, it acquired a factory in Malaysia to help it expand into the Far East market.

In the automobile industry, **BorgWarner (NYSE: BWA)**, with a market capitalisation of $3.6 billion in mid-2009, is also highly sensitive towards the energy-efficiency theme both for higher fuel efficiency and for lower emissions. Traditionally known for its car gearboxes, a sector it has now left, BorgWarner's key products are all aimed at higher fuel efficiency and lower emissions and account for over 80% of its revenues. BorgWarner is active in auto-fuel efficiency, performance enhancement and emission reduction, having expertise in engine timing, turbochargers, ignition technology, emission systems, cooling and air and noise management. It also has over 100 years of experience in railway engine technologies. The company, which was formed by a merger in 1928, employs 17,700 people worldwide and recorded $289 million in net earnings in 2007 from sales to most major auto companies in Europe (49%), North America (31%) and Asia (20%).

Johnson Matthey PLC (London: JMAT), with a market capitalisation of £2.5 billion in mid-2009, is a specialist chemical business in catalysis, precious metals, fine chemicals and process technology. It is a joint leader in auto catalysts with 31% global market share and has over 40% market share in diesel technology, especially for trucks and buses. JMAT's main activities are in the manufacture of auto catalysts, heavy-duty catalysts, fuel-cell catalysts and pollution control systems. JMAT, which has operations in over thirty countries and employs 8,700 people worldwide, is well positioned to benefit from growth in diesel engine market share, especially in the USA, where only 4% of light-duty vehicles are diesel compared to 50% in Europe.

Spirax Sarco (London: SPX) is a Cheltenham-based, medium-sized company with a market capitalisation of £640 million in mid-2009 and is the market leader in products designed to improve industrial efficiency in the use of steam, which is primarily used to drive turbines to create electricity. Spirax Sarco's products include steam traps, temperature and pressure controls, pumps and pipeline ancillaries that cost little relative to the savings they generate. It is also the world's largest manufacturer of peristaltic tube and hose pumps that have no valves, seals or glands and are used widely across the chemical, pharmaceutical and biotechnology industries to enable sensitive, abrasive or corrosive fluids to be pumped safely. Spirax Sarco is a pure play on energy efficiency as a service provider.

Utilities

Lighting accounts for about 20% of global electricity consumption, but the conventional incandescent bulb is highly inefficient, wasting most of its input energy in the form of heat with only 5% of the electricity used for light, leading to a large shift into energy-saving light bulbs, compact fluorescent bulbs or LED solutions.

The winner in the lighting market will be light-emitting diodes (LEDs). While currently the high brightness of LEDs emitting white light is used in niche applications, it is likely to drive into the mass market very quickly, replacing the dominant new player, the compact fluorescent light bulb, after reductions in LEDs' higher manufacturing costs come into play. LEDs have lower power consumption because of their highly efficient conversion of energy into light and, consequently, their lower consumption of energy, requiring less voltage and almost zero maintenance. They have an extremely long life of 100,000 hours (eleven years). Currently, LED technology is used in mobile devices, notebooks and LCD TVs, but it has inevitably been moving into the residential market where the greatest energy efficiencies can be realised.

Cree Inc. (NASDAQ: CREE), with a mid-2009 market value of $2.7 billion, was formed in 1987 by a group of researchers from North Carolina State University and is the world leader in the development and manufacture of silicon carbide, the base material used in the fabrication of its product range, which includes LED chips, lamps for signs, indicators and general lighting and power components for motor drive and hybrid electric engines. It is the only exclusive LED player among the top five in the LED sector and hence has a 100% exposure to energy efficiency. Cree was one of the few quoted companies in the world that grew in value between 2008 and 2009.

Epistar Corp. (Taiwan: 2448TW), valued by the market in mid-2009 at €1.2 billion, is a leading LED chip manufacturer. Founded in 1996, Epistar develops, manufactures and markets LED products designed using the company's in-house technology. Its products are compact, have low energy consumption and a long operational life, and are used in applications such as scanners, automobile lighting, indoor and outdoor displays and traffic signals. Like Cree, Epistar also defied market trends and grew in value between 2008 and 2009.

Plug Power Inc. (NASDAQ: PLUG), with a market capitalisation of $250 million in mid-2009, is a company that manufactures a number of products for fuel cells and fuel-processing systems designed to improve backup power as an alternative to batteries. Plug Power's GenDrive system offers an alternative to lead-acid batteries for motive power. The company also has a product known as GenSys, which is an application for storing power off grid that promises to deliver lower maintenance and fuel cost, lower emissions and less noise compared to the traditional combustion engine.

Peerless Manufacturing Co. (NASDAQ: PMFG), with a market capitalisation of $75 million in mid-2009, manufactures a specialised catalytic reduction system used to clean gases and air by removing solid and liquid by-products and emissions as they pass through piping systems. It has a special application in cleaning the exhaust from coal, petroleum, natural gas and oil-fired power stations, converting the damaging nitrogen oxide emissions into harmless nitrogen and water. It also specialises in removing contaminants from natural gas and is well positioned in the fast developing market to reduce CO_2 emissions and avoid carbon taxes. Remember, levying carbon tax is at a very early stage globally, and as regulation permeates through economies, carbon trading is likely to become a major global market.

EnerNOC Inc. (NASDAQ: ENOC), quoted on the NASDAQ with a market capitalisation of $450 million in mid-2009, is a company that provides smart systems to commercial customers to help them regulate and lower their electricity supply costs by monitoring demand loads on the electricity grid. EnerNOC builds and manages a network between the end-user and the electricity grid that curtails the load when utilities and grid operators face supply constraints. This curtailment produces 'negawatts' that relieve pressure on the grid by reducing electricity demand, instead of the electricity supply company having to add to generation capacity.

Itron Inc. (NASDAQ: ITRI), with a market capitalisation of $2 billion in mid-2009, controls over 50% of the US smart metering marketplace. Unlike the old analogue electric meters, which have to be checked by a meter reader, smart meters are sophisticated devices that can be read remotely by an electricity supply company while also providing useful feedback to customers on their energy consumption patterns. Itron Inc. is a leader in the provision of meters for electricity, water, heat and gas, using a combination of hardware and software as well as providing consultancy and support to its customers. Itron provides the metering technology, collects the data, and provides management and analytic services designed to improve energy efficiency.

Beacon Power (NASDAQ: BECON), with a market capitalisation in mid-2009 of $87 million, designs and develops flywheel power systems that provide uninterruptible electric power for its customers. Beacon's solar inverters boost energy independence and promote renewable power. Its solutions are designed to deliver instant power from solar energy systems or from backup batteries in the event of a power failure. Beacon has a patented advanced composite flywheel technology that helps store energy, and its primary business is to commercialise this innovation.

Transport

Hydrogen is the Harry Houdini of elements, as its tiny particles will try to escape out of just about anything and it boils into its gaseous state at $-252.87°C$. Proponents of a hydrogen-fuelled economy fail to apply EROEI when visualising a future in which hydrogen, which does not exist freely, can be liberated from a source and blended with oxygen in a fuel cell to throw off energy and create water. The process requires large inputs of energy, typically from gas, and there is substantial leakage when the element is compressed into liquid form, when it is stored and when it is transported as a fuel for cars.

A hydrogen economy would also require a vast change in infrastructure globally, involving piping grids, new service-station pumps and new vehicles. The most likely future transportation fuel is electricity in plug-in hybrid electric vehicles (PHEVs), especially as battery technology evolves. Already electricity is revolutionising train transport, as in the French TGV, for example, which whisks along at over 200 miles per hour. Electric railways dominate new rail development in Europe and Japan. The biggest market for growth is probably the USA, which is already seeing large increases in railway journeys as pump prices rise and Americans ditch their cars in favour of the train.

Conventional railway companies may not seem as racy as other investments in energy efficiency, but, as oil prices increase, rail's share of the transport market will grow, so there's money to be made. In many European countries, rail businesses are publicly owned and therefore unavailable to investors, but not so in the USA where there has been a long and venerable tradition of private companies involved in building and running the vast US rail network.

Burlington Northern Santa Fe (NYSE: BNI), with a market capitalisation of $23 billion in mid-2008, is the outcome of 390 different rail companies that merged or were acquired over the past 150 years. BNSF had 11% of its stock acquired by Warren Buffett's Berkshire Hathaway Inc. in 2007 – and he usually knows a good thing when he sees it. At the close of 2009 Buffett made the biggest move of his career to fully acquire the railway for $26.3 billion. The US media made much guff about Buffett's big bet on the US economy, but Buffett was really buying into peak oil, betting that rapidly rising fuel costs would switch huge numbers of automobile drivers on to his trains.

Canadian National Railway (Toronto/NYSE: CNI), into which another canny entrepreneur, Bill Gates of Microsoft fame, is heavily invested, had a market capitalisation of $19.5 billion in mid-2009. Founded in 1830, Canadian National Railway crisscrosses North America with more than 20,000 route-miles of track, over ten times more than Ireland's state-owned Iarnród Éireann. It is the only carrier on the North American continent that covers east–west and north–south routes, serving ports on the Atlantic, Pacific and Gulf coasts, and is therefore well positioned to attract new business on rising petrol prices.

10. Probabilities and Possibilities

So, now that you're nearing the end of *Energise*, what do you think is the most likely outcome for the decades ahead? The depletion of fossil fuels, especially oil and gas, is pretty much a given. Will technological improvements like horizontal drilling, breakthroughs like SulphCo's process to improve crude-oil quality and intensive drilling in hard locations like the deep seas and the Arctic be enough to outpace embedded global demand growth for energy? Will a new green industrial revolution spring from the transition from fossil fuels, especially given the enormous scope to save energy costs by driving forward improvements in energy efficiency? After all, if we can go from 30 mpg cars to 100 mpg in a matter of a few years, what else is possible to string out fossil-fuel supplies and buy more time to find replacements? The big question is: will it be enough and what happens if we simply run out of time, invention and affordable energy?

Huge improvements in energy-efficiency technology and processes such as smart metering and fuel cells will deploy in mature OECD economies, reducing overall energy demand, but will this compensate for the inevitable increase in demand from fast-growing developing economies like the BRIC group? It's an economic truth that increases in efficiency don't necessarily lead to decreased consumption but, paradoxically, can increase consumption. This has been the story of oil so far. The cheaper oil becomes, the more addicted to it we become.

Spikes in oil prices depress economic growth, leading to lower demand for oil and energy-efficiency drives. The result is oil prices falling sharply, lending credence to those oil proponents who say that depletion is a myth. We return to a business-as-usual mentality with cheaper oil, demand grows again and the cycle is repeated, except this time the spike is higher. When oil has passed peak, the likelihood is a series of spikes until we hit a point of rapid depletion, a tipping point beyond which there's unlikely to be enough energy, money or time left to replace oil.

That's what some gloomier analysts argue. But maybe, like me, you're an optimist. I'd like to think that a multitude of breakthroughs will come, that sufficient capital and human invention will arrive in time to save us from the worst-case scenario, but you can't plan for success without understanding the ramifications of failure. That's why oil alarmists have a vital role to play in warning us of the dangers on our doorstep and we dismiss their expert analysis at our peril.

But already the signs are there that scientists, engineers, academics and R&D divisions of muscular commercial organisations are galvanising around energy security as it moves to the top of government agendas worldwide. It's a far cry from just a few short years ago when, with oil at under $30 a barrel, 'peakers' were dismissed as nutcases. So I wouldn't be too quick to bet against human ingenuity, when it is sufficiently focused on a challenge of this scale. That's where I'd place my money and the future of my own children.

This isn't just wishful thinking, but reasoning that some of the worst-case scenarios put forward by doomsayers have certain holes in them. For starters, much of the darker analysis assumes that a cut in our current usage of energy would be fatal, but this ignores the huge scope for efficiency gains. Let's face it, we haven't really been properly challenged just yet and continue to waste vast amounts of energy in unnecessary travel, gas-guzzling transport, food miles, luxury lighting … the list goes on and on. Secondly, energy is hugely taxed in nearly every country other than oil-producing nations, so a shift in the tax burden to other methods of revenue raising could be used to dampen runaway prices and buy time. Thirdly there's the X-factor, the impact of invention and of an accelerated switch to alternatives to oil and gas as those alternatives become increasingly affordable. This crossover point hasn't been reached yet, but has the potential to spark a new green industrial revolution, especially now that the world is interconnected and interdependent both economically and socially through the internet – the most revolutionary invention since the steam engines sparked the industrial revolution. Fourthly, doomsayers assume that the energy we need to fire such a revolution is incremental energy, in other words, on top of what we're already using. This ignores the impact of redirecting existing energy use to new technologies, like car makers switching current electricity costs to the production of electric vehicles and trains.

But part of the deal in talking about oil is to peer into the chasm, the dark side of peaking, to understand what happens if we don't get these things just right.

Let me just say that, although I'll point out some possible results from the forces now unleashed, it does not mean these scenarios are going to happen, nor do I wish for such results. Far from it, I hope that scalable and transportable alternatives to oil will be found and that the vast gains in energy efficiency combined with the growth in renewables will do the trick. Neither can you entirely rule out 'black swans', seismic and totally unexpected developments that forever change how we do things. What can be said with reasonable certainty is that the best-case scenario is a long-term period of turbulence in global economic conditions as oil prices behave erratically, but where the underlying trend is sharply upwards.

Let's remember, oil is an unsurpassed source of energy, storing more power by weight and volume than any other substance except nuclear feedstock. Oil is easily stored, easily transported across the world, easy to pump and, unless you're a complete chucklehead, it is reasonably safe to handle. Oil is the reason the world population is heading towards 7 billion; it is cheap and its widespread availability has facilitated globalisation, delivering the benefits of industrialised agriculture, cars, electrified homes, air conditioning, heating and countless white goods and services to billions of consumers throughout the world.

The depletion of oil without a sustainable substitute would cause economic and social reversal on a scale and at a pace unseen in the history of mankind. At its imperial peak, the population of Rome stood at about 1 million, but by the time industrialisation began in the mid-1700s, Rome's population had shrunk by around 90%. But even the combined falls of the Roman, Mayan and Sumerian empires would pale into insignificance against the fall of economic empires throughout the world this century if oil were to deplete without scalable replacements. Thankfully, emergency breeds invention.

The Manhattan Project

The pressing need to defeat Japanese and German expansionism during the Second World War created the last great intensive scientific exploration for a new source of energy. The legacy of the Manhattan Project, which involved pulling together a team of top scientists, giving it a deadline and a near bottomless budget, was nuclear power, the frightening down payment of which was the destruction of two Japanese populations in Nagasaki and Hiroshima. But there have been no major discoveries since, nothing yet on the supply side of the equation to replace fossil fuels. Work on nuclear fusion, the energy released by fusing two hydrogen atoms to create helium, which is the process upon which the hydrogen bomb is based, is no closer to controlling and harnessing the energy created than it was during the 1970s. French research seems most advanced, but breakthroughs aren't expected until mid-century, if at all.

Understandable popular resistance to the expansion of nuclear fission has simply deepened our addiction to oil. Despite the inevitability of depleting our resources of fossil fuels, many countries have followed the American lead of building sprawling urban centres extending out hundreds of miles from gargantuan skyscrapers and pursuing a lifestyle that's entirely predicated on access to cheap energy simply to get about.

I remember holidaying in Texas, Arizona, California and Florida over a period extending from the 1980s to 2006 and I was struck by the distances US citizens drive to get to just about anything. On my last holiday, which was in Florida, we seemed to spend an inordinate amount of time in the car zipping hither and thither for minor things. The USA is built for the car. US motorists are estimated to use their cars twice as much as Europeans and travel four times the distance. A lot of US car travel is to out-of-town, big-box shopping malls, just to get stuff. Food, on average, travels 1,100 miles from farm to fork in the US and daily commutes to work of 100 miles are normal.

If you think about it, we've moved from localisation to globalisation very rapidly, but it's all based on access to affordable and transportable fuel. Ireland has made the leap from being a closed organic agricultural society to one dependent on industrialised agriculture and global trade, especially for services, in just forty years. Meanwhile, Dublin has sprawled out fifty miles in most directions.

The dark side

It would be intellectually dishonest not to examine the possibility of global economic collapse because of a failure to engage adequately, with sufficient resources and in sufficient time, with oil depletion. So let's begin our journey into a possible time when the lights start to go out by understanding what needs to be done.

Ireland is hugely dependent on imported oil and gas. Consider what would happen if the supply dried up or was slashed as geopolitical tension escalated to a point where the nations of the earth scrambled for freely available energy sources. What happens if Israel attacks the embryonic Iranian nuclear power assets and Iran responds by choking the Strait of Hormuz? With 60% of the world oil supply threatened, a US-led coalition would probably invade Iran to reopen supply lines. But how long would that take and what would be the strategic response of other players, like Russia and China? In 1999, Dick Cheney, the CEO of Halliburton, estimated a 5% gap opening between oil supply and demand. Three years later, and by now as US Vice President, Cheney linked US foreign policy to energy. Shortly after that, US troops in Baghdad found no weapons of mass destruction, but plenty of cheap oil.

It's clear that the removal of the despot Saddam Hussein, who was in defiance of UN resolutions, doubled as cover for the start of the energy wars. Strategically, the US required a presence within the oil-rich Gulf, so that it would be poised to enter Saudi Arabia, which holds a quarter of the world's oil reserves, at a moment's notice. This would add to the US's encirclement of Iran, which holds the area's second largest reserves, with forces east and west in Iraq and Afghanistan, north in Azerbaijan, Uzbekistan, Kyrgyzstan and Tajikistan and naval forces to the south in the Persian Gulf. If the US-led invasion of Iraq wasn't principally about oil then pigs, rhinoceroses and elephants can fly.

In 2008, Russia, under the cover of protecting South Ossetia from Georgian aggression, started its own energy war by invading neighbouring Georgia to the south. Georgia and the Ukraine, which also feels threatened, are at the strategic crossroads between central Asian oil and gas supply lines and the West, including the US and Europe. The pipeline that traverses Georgia carries 1% of global oil supplies from Baku in Azerbaijan on the Caspian Sea 1,100 miles to Ceyhan on the Turkish coast, bypassing Russia to the north and Iran to the south. Russia, which has already used its gas pipeline through the Ukraine to flex its muscles, sent another shivering reminder to oil- and gas-dependent regions, especially Europe and the US, that control of energy is the trump card.

How would Ireland cope without a stable and reliable oil and gas supply? Under agreements with the IEA, Ireland has just three months' oil in a national reserve for which it pays 1 cent for every litre sold. A 20% fall in Irish oil supplies would trigger a package of demand restraint measures under the Irish Fuels (Control of Supplies) Acts 1972 and 1982, including speed limits, traffic restrictions, alternate driving days for private cars, petrol and diesel rationing at stations, restricted opening hours, limitations on deliveries to domestic and commercial oil-storage tanks, a ban on sales in containers and cans supported by a national advertising campaign and penalties for non-compliance. The national oil reserve would be targeted at essential services, which Irish readers will be glad to know includes members of the Oireachtas and their three-month summer holiday!

Even if Irish green energy targets are reached by 2020, the country will still be 60% dependent on fossil fuels to heat homes, run factories, grow crops and transport food. Irish wind, tidal and biofuel energy industries are built on oil foundations. Wind turbines are notorious for breaking down and will need spare parts – which will be manufactured where? Supplying more turbines needs steel and transport from manufacturing operations in Europe. These can't be made or transported using wind-generated electricity. Bio-crops would need to be harvested on a mass scale using specialised equipment that would have to be manufactured, imported and maintained.

Perhaps you've already concluded that most alternative energy sources aren't alternative at all, but merely complementary to existing energy sources. Each to some degree or another is inextricably linked to oil and global trade.

Some argue that Ireland is protected by its EU membership and the plans for Europe-wide electrical interconnectivity, but the country sits at the furthermost edge of the proposed European supply grid, which is anyway many years from completion. Furthermore, Europe itself is hugely dependent on imported energy, including gas from an aggressive Russia, which has threatened Poland, an EU member, with a nuclear strike. In the event of pan-European rationing of energy, how well do you think Irish diplomats would fare in the teeth of competition from countries closer to external energy supply lines? Let's face it, Ireland is at heightened risk of economic collapse in the event of an oil crunch. Consider the political and social turmoil that would arise as shops ran out of sufficient food supplies. Ireland is a net exporter of home-grown meat and foodstuffs, but each of these exists on an oil platform. Agriculture has long since been industrialised. Oil powers the machinery that harvests crops and transports food to the shops. A prolonged energy emergency would propel Ireland back several generations. The world would change from globalisation to localisation and the EU would not hold under the strain.

Communities would need to reorganise to a more simplified society around local needs and resources. Many jobs would cease to be required as labour shifted to manual agriculture. The top demand of Irish society would, once again, be to produce food, putting at least a third of the workforce on farms to feed the other two-thirds.

Yep, it's a pretty shocking scenario, but just how elevated are the risks that it could come to pass? Much like climate change, as fossil-fuel depletion gains a foothold in popular belief, the world will either co-operate in solving its energy demands, including curbing population growth, or it will disintegrate into regionalised groups competing against each other. So where are the geopolitical fault lines?

Geopolitics

Tension between Iran and US-backed Israel is evident, as are the risks it brings unless some form of agreement can be reached about Iranian plans to produce nuclear power and its potential to make nuclear weapons. But as the world cottons on to oil depletion, while energy demand grows, everything that depends on oil will come under enormous strain: trade, transport, manufacturing, agriculture and the financial markets that support them. Meanwhile, on the ground, Islamic nations, who control the bulk of global oil reserves to which the rest of the world is addicted, are hostile to their largest customer, the US.

As oil-producing nations pass their peak, power will concentrate in three countries as the swing producers: Saudi Arabia, Kuwait and Iraq. Then they too will peak. Look beyond the overarching issue of hostility to Israel, which acts as a useful vent for frustration, and the Arab world is seething with internal tensions. It's hard to see how Saudi Arabia can survive intact in the control of the 30,000-strong al-Saud clan who oversee Wahhabism, an extreme type of Islam, and administer a brutally repressive regime while themselves enjoying vast riches and opulent lifestyles. History has taught us that such regimes eventually topple, and the risk is that the al-Saud clan will topple to extremists rather than to modernists and reformers. Most jobs in Saudi Arabia are taken up by foreigners, leaving many young Saudi men with the choice of unemployment or Islamic studies. Effectively, the Saudi government, while propping up a multitude of playboy princes who get their kicks abroad, is financing the seeds of its own destruction. It's only a question of when it happens. How the Kingdom, which conducts the highest number of public beheadings in the world, has managed to survive intact so far is something of a mystery.

A Saudi Arabia threatening to unravel to al-Qaeda extremists would pose unique problems to the US, which is already stretched trying to keep the lid on hostility within Iraq. Even if the US invaded the Arabian Peninsula it would be unable to hold it, never mind the damage the conflict would cause to the region's oil pipelines, infrastructure and, consequently, supply.

Regional failure by the US, even if supported by Europe, would create a unique opportunity for China, geographically closer to the Middle East than the US and with no track record to upset local sensitivities. China, entering the game late as the last great oil economy with a population double that of the US and Europe combined, militarily has the capacity to guarantee security to nearby central Asian states and to extend its influence as far as the Middle East, creating a new Great Game in which the pieces on the chess board are not expansionist ideologies but pressures at home to avoid disintegration because of energy shortages, which will be especially acute for the Chinese.

Russia, having already flexed its muscle in the Caucuses, may not be a net exporter for too much longer. Russia passed its own oil peak in the 1980s and will find itself facing similar problems to the US in the years to come.

Whichever way you look at oil depletion, without scalable replacements it's hard not to conceive of energy conflicts erupting as major world powers, losing their capacity to extend their influence overseas, become forced to retract, to deal with maintaining power at home as energy supplies wane and social unrest grows. The Chinese, whose imported energy demand is rapidly changing the face of the international market, face an equally enormous challenge with water. Over half of China's 617 cities already face water shortages, as groundwater levels fall sharply because supplies are being diverted to ever more intensive agriculture.

The poorest nations will be hardest hit in the chequebook economics that will emerge as oil depletes. But already over half of the world's population live in urban housing, many of them in the vast sprawling slums extending out from traditional city centres. As depletion bites the outlook for these poorest regions is as grim as it would be for health systems worldwide, unable to cope with mass killers like SARS and AIDS and the others which will follow if the fight between microbiology and superbugs is lost owing to lack of resources.

How would Ireland cope with depletion?

Remember, the scenario here is based on oil depletion without compensating measures, such as scalable replacements and energy-efficiency drives. Firstly, you have to be practical and ask yourself what would Irish society keep and what would it shed as it became increasingly localised? Secondly, failing a sudden and destructive war in the Middle East that laid waste to its oil infrastructure, depletion will occur slowly. Its drip, drip effect would be punctuated by periods of economic boom and bust, before depletion set in proper, giving Irish society some time to reorganise after emerging from an inevitable prolonged period of denial that times had changed permanently, wealth had disappeared, especially in urban property markets, and jobs had become redundant, along with large-scale industry.

Large complex systems, reliant on oil-driven industrialised agriculture, with long supply lines stretching from Latin America and New Zealand to Ireland, would end, as would the multinational corporate model that relies on managing assets across vast distances, from cheap labour in developing economies to sophisticated high-cost consumers in mature ones.

Its little consolation, but some regions would be worse off than Ireland. Arid, highly urbanised parts of the US that have flourished only because of massive irrigation systems and cheap transport would be hit hard and become largely uninhabitable. Europe would fare a little better since most countries did not give up farming around city hinterlands quite to the same degree the US did. Ireland, with its temperate climate, agricultural heritage and wind energy potential, is fortunate, but it would still face enormous challenges.

First and foremost would be the requirement to feed the population from agricultural processes increasingly reliant on manual farming, knowledge of which would have been lost save for organic farmers, smallholders and leisure farmers. Once again, good land would become the premium asset as survival became the primary goal of society. Localised niches would open up to add value to the chain, such as butchers, cheese makers and delivery services. Shops would revert from large, town-edge supermarkets to independent local traders, since the economies of scale enjoyed from long, overseas supply lines by Tesco, Dunnes and other players would evaporate. Easy-to-peel sweeter Australian oranges would disappear from the shelves along with a host of other imports. The working-horse population would see a revival as mechanical horsepower was replaced by its four-legged forebear for ploughing, harvesting and other agricultural chores. Communities would begin to organise basic services locally, especially energy supply. Micro generators based on creating electricity from domestic and community wind turbines, rivers and streams and biomass would be used to supplement an unstable national grid. Large parts of Irish suburbia would become ghost towns, as the population shifted to the traditional rural centres favoured by pre-industrial Irish society.

Salvaging and repairs would become big business as international manufacturing supply lines extending from China, Korea and Japan closed down. Material from unutilised property would be the principal source of building, and repair skills and services would grow as the ability to replace products diminished. Traditional skills such as carpentry, metalwork and stonemasonry would become highly prized and, much to the dismay of liberals, society would return to more traditional roles where having a large family became economically desirable as more children entered the workforce as apprentices.

Even if oil were to end, living standards would remain far ahead of those of the 1800s. Much that has been learned in the interim would not be lost. Society would continue to need professionals like doctors, dentists, nurses, teachers, police, undertakers and, God forbid, even solicitors and bankers, but much will be on a local scale. It's hard to see how complex multinational organisations like the EU and its single currency could survive intact if politics were to become intensely localised. National government structures would cede much authority to municipalities and community organisations. Some currencies like the euro would localise, most likely backed by precious metals.

There would still be energy, especially nuclear electricity from those countries that possess nuclear assets. Energy would be created nationally and locally, but nothing remotely on the scale necessary to support Irish society as it is now organised. Maintaining the integrity of the electricity supply and the grid would be a real challenge.

What can be done to prepare?

Remember, economic collapse isn't written in stone; it's just the inevitable outcome if we screw up the future. It is more likely that the combination of vast growth in energy efficiency, the development of new and existing energy sources and the human capacity to invent will provide a safety net, but only after a prolonged period of economic turbulence. Sky-high oil prices, however, will certainly change the world as we know it. Globalisation, a handy word to describe the stripping and relocation of manufacture to the cheapest labour markets, will begin to reverse. World trade will shift dramatically as transport costs, especially for heavy items like steel, furniture and food, make moving goods huge distances unviable. Traditional industries will return and with them new jobs. As CO_2 emission costs bite, the US, Europe and Japan will be forced to apply carbon tariffs on imports from economies that are generating products using dirty energy, levelling the playing field on which local manufacturers and foreign companies compete. A green China will quickly emerge. Local markets will become much more important and land around cities will be converted back to producing food. Irish orchards will make a welcome comeback, as will allotments for rent by enterprising farmers. You can whistle goodbye to New Zealand lamb, flowers from Indonesia and just about anything that relies on travelling huge distances under refrigeration. Massive investment in public transport will accompany the huge shift from inefficient gas guzzlers to electric cars. The death and reinvention of the US auto industry is already underway. This is just the beginning. Long-distance flights will become a rarity except for the rich as tourism also localises.

Whatever the outcome, it would be madness not to prepare. The best strategy is to take a twin-track approach. Plan A, recast your own balance sheet to invest in assets that are positively correlated to scarcity prices for oil and other natural resources, invest in alternative energy and in energy efficiency. But be ready with Plan B if, globally, we fail to respond in time and on a sufficient scale to meet the depletion challenge. Plan B is for another book by another writer, but it involves taking your profits and buying land, investing in pre-oil-age assets and learning how to grow food, manage farm animals and meet the needs of a localised marketplace. Alien as it may sound, you can make a start on your own Plan B now, by investing in better insulation and learning how to grow your own vegetables, manage your own allotment, repair your own equipment and even rear your own hens!

But Ireland hasn't yet arrived at a point where oil depletion is remotely accepted as a given. It needs a kick in the backside to start a public debate about our vulnerability and why our renewable energy targets are simply not good enough. What is needed is a fundamental rethink, a new energy strategy and action plan that combine the resources of the state and private enterprise in a race to prepare for a disruption to international fossil-fuel supplies.

Ireland enjoys considerable geographical advantages; it has the potential to become a world leader in wind and wave energy, and can combine these to support hydro-storage reservoirs. Insufficient urgency and an absence of incentives look like guaranteeing that Ireland will fail to prepare in time, but that can be changed by acting on a number of fronts. For openers, the cornerstone of infrastructural investment in future budgets needs to be refocused on an Irish quest for energy security. Energy has to be on the tip of everyone's tongue and has to dominate political and local business agendas, because nothing else will work without sufficient energy supplies. In parallel, Irish government policy needs to incentivise invention in energy efficiency technologies, combining corporate and academic resources.

But Ireland also needs to invest in Plan B by incentivising local organic food production, distribution and markets, and by adding to the school curriculum practical and traditional skills that will help equip our children for what's to come in the Age of Scarcity, when DIY, repairs, food production and animal husbandry may become more important than preparing for an MBA.

Transport policy needs urgent change, redeploying more spending towards a future of electric trains and cars. Irish waterways and canals need to be reopened. Ireland needs to plan for the best but prepare for the worst over the decades ahead.

Nuclear Ireland?

There's the inevitable but ugly question of whether we can afford not to go nuclear, a strategy that now can be countered by the Spirit of Ireland model outlined below.

Nuclear proponents will argue that while, in the past, we rejected nuclear power, that decision was made at a time of oil abundance. This time, it's very different. Faced with the choice of going nuclear or managing economic decline, what would we do? Anti-nuclear proponents point accurately to the hidden cost of nuclear waste and the inadequate scale of the Irish grid in coping with nuclear reactors that would be out of commission at least 15% of the time for refuelling and maintenance. But these arguments have not been re-examined since the first evidence of oil and gas depletion presented itself.

The Finns have had their debate and gone nuclear to supplement hydropower. In France, EDF, the electricity monopoly, supplies up to 80% of electricity from nuclear power plants and is just adding a new 1,600MW plant in northern France which will take seven years to construct. Chernobyl, which melted down on 26 April 1986, is used as the common argument for rejection, but the Chernobyl plant was an old Soviet reactor that ignored at least a dozen safety protocols, including not having a containment shell. In short, it was an accident waiting to happen. The Soviets' incompetent design, which triggered an increase in the reaction rate if the reactor overheated, led to a death toll in the low thousands, a swathe of uninhabitable land and a marked increase in cancer deaths in the surrounding region.

Chernobyl aside, the track record of the nuclear industry globally over the fifty years of its existence has been a remarkably safe one. In a world facing oil and gas depletion and based on current technologies, proponents will argue that the only plausible way to sustain electricity supplies, including those necessary to run electric cars and trains, is by combining renewable energy with nuclear power. One possible alternative, and one I've been exploring closely with colleagues, would be to build an electricity interconnector between Ireland and France, with electricity priced at the

French electricity market pool rate plus the cost of interconnection. In turn, at times when there is excess wind electricity generated in Ireland, green power could be exported to France.

In the times ahead, great wealth and long-term sustainable advantage will accrue to any nation that can meet its own energy needs and export surplus energy from non-fossil-fuel sources to neighbouring countries that face supply deficits. Could Ireland become an energy powerhouse? The answer is yes, the objective is strategically sound, but could it be achieved without having a nuclear power station on the island?

Hydro-storage Ireland?

Energise was originally to have a different ending, one designed to set off alarm bells in political circles in an attempt to shake off the lethargy about what is to come, perhaps even reopening the old sores of the nuclear debate. Such a wake-up call from me has become less imperative following the advent of a possible solution from Spirit of Ireland that combines wind power and hydropower. This opens up the possibility of energy independence within a few years and the tantalising prospect that Ireland will become a net green energy exporter. From a standing start of 90% dependence on volatile international oil and gas markets, such a turnaround would be stunning. I'm not expert enough to measure the validity of such a claim at this early point, but I do believe that the Spirit of Ireland proposition needs to be given wholehearted consideration and research, and that, for the time being, we should park aside the natural reaction to be dismissive.

In April 2009, after sounding off again on radio about why we must urgently elevate energy to the top national priority and consider importing nuclear electricity from France via an interconnector, I received a remarkable phone call from a seasoned entrepreneur, Graham O'Donnell, an electrical engineer by profession and an independently wealthy businessman who knows how to get things done. Heading up the Spirit of Ireland project team with Professor Igor Svets of Trinity College and several other highly qualified professionals, Graham outlined an extraordinary plan to solve Ireland's inevitable future energy crisis. Already subject to detailed research by leading international and Irish experts, the plan is to focus Ireland's growing wind energy assets to pumping sea-water from the Atlantic into high-altitude, shallow and U-shaped gorges, thereby creating hydropower reservoirs. Sites have already been identified. This novel breakthrough in thinking occurred when Professor Svets had been hill walking in the West of Ireland and he considered how a similar project in Okinawa could be replicated there.

The Spirit of Ireland project team point out that Ireland spends €3 billion each year on imported oil and gas, that's €30 billion leaving the country to fossil-fuel-rich nations over ten years, even if Irish energy demands remain static. Consider the cost as oil and gas prices rise. According to the team's research, the base load of 3,500MW and peak load of 7,000MW could be met by a number of hydro-storage reservoirs fed by over 2,000 wind turbines. Self-evidently, detailed economic modelling will be needed, and the cost of upgrading Ireland's electricity distribution network taken into account. This is expected to run to €4 billion over fifteen years, but could potentially fall to less than €1 billion if the proposed network is redrawn to support a small number of hydro-storage reservoirs instead of scattering countrywide to meet the current dubious plan to feed wind energy directly into the grid. Economists will need to ignore previous IEA estimates on future fossil-fuel prices and run sensitivity analysis on what happens when prices sky rocket and the proposed network of open-cycle gas turbines have to make up the deficit caused by periods of no wind.

The Spirit of Ireland strategy, if it stands up to independent scrutiny, could solve the central weakness of wind power – its intermittency – by converting wind power to much more reliable hydropower. Ownership of the reservoirs would rest with the Irish people through a public company with finance supplied by ethical investment from Sovereign Wealth Funds and pension funds. Wind turbine investors, mostly small farmer co-ops on or near the western seaboard, would be remunerated through a fixed tariff, devised to help them recover set-up costs over a ten-year cycle with pre-packaged banking finance. The impact on foreign direct investment in the country would be profound if Ireland were to achieve this extraordinary ambition to become the first country in the world to be energy independent, with most of its self-generated supply based on renewable sources producing stable electricity prices with very low carbon costs.

Provided that the business plan and the science, which is based on proven technologies, both stack up, this is an idea worth serious exploration and analysis, but one which faces embedded obstacles from vested interests and from state sluggishness in preparing the ground. For starters, there's the question of Ireland's obsolete grid. In reality, this largely comprises a distribution network of low-efficiency cables with little by way of the modern grid technology that other countries enjoy. This crumbling and antiquated infra-structure means Ireland's electricity demand growth cannot be met. The solution is to fast track upgrading the grid to a network of high-voltage cables, which is currently envisaged by EirGrid to take place by 2025.

But even though Ireland's independent grid operator has been in place for several years now, EirGrid still doesn't own the grid, which remains on the balance sheet of the Electricity Supply Board. This chasm is mired in the politics of self-interest and must be tackled urgently if new energy development of any scale is to be delivered to businesses and consumers. Secondly, the scheme needs a co-ordinated response from government with a package of incentives and measures to encourage faster development of wind assets and to focus these within the strategic collection areas around the proposed reservoirs. Finally, the thorny issue of planning delays has to be tackled once and for all to prevent development of key national projects becoming bogged down by spurious objections, especially objections to high-voltage power lines. That requires adjusting legislation and introducing community incentives to co-operate with the inevitable development of a new electricity grid across key lines throughout the country.

Ireland's hydro-storage assets cannot expand and fulfil the ambition to export electricity without a network of commercial interconnectors to Britain and France, where credits for green energy will become hugely attractive to those countries' electricity market pools. That means corresponding supports for more interconnectors, especially those linking directly to the European continent. On the political front, the plan proposed by Fine Gael's policy think tank contains a refreshing and ambitious strategy to reform and refocus state companies on an integrated range of themes, including broadband, water, greener homes and, tellingly, renewable energy, bio-energy and smart metering. Called NewERA, it proposes to boost spending on these sectors by a further €11 billion, financed by the National Pensions Reserve Fund, bond issues and the European Investment Bank and to be repaid by levying charges on the economic growth created over several decades. It's a daring and radical plan, not just because it contains savvy ideas but because it involves utilising state companies as the delivery vehicles under the aegis of a new, overarching and all-powerful state-run recovery company. That's why it's daring. It faces into the headwinds of resistance from a public sector that embraces sluggishness, conservativeness and inefficiencies.

It doesn't take much thinking to foresee the barriers that will be placed before the Spirit of Ireland initiative or Fine Gael's New-ERA strategy from embedded players, including electricity providers like the ESB and labour cartels like the public-sector unions which regard reform as open season for pay hikes. Neither does it take too much more reasoning to expect the machinery of the state and its political system to react at a snail's pace, despite the glaringly open window of opportunity to secure the assets necessary at depressed prices during the global recession. Delay will mean much higher costs for everything from steel components for wind turbines to the concrete and copper needed to build the infrastructure.

Become a lightning rod

So perhaps that wake-up call is still needed, after all. That's why one of the appendices to *Energise* contains the email address of every elected representative in the 30th Dáil. If there's one thing I've learned from getting political momentum going, it's that the response is in direct proportion to the size of the mailbag from the public. Remember, the Groceries Order was taken down four years ago by flooding the Department of Enterprise and Employment with nappies, which were listed for artificial price protection as a grocery! If the Groceries Order was in place today, the price war between retailers would be illegal since passing on supplier discounts was banned.

Few politicians understood or cared about grocery prices until they became a very public issue. Today, most of them have no understanding of the jeopardy we face and the huge opportunities we can grasp if we act on time. You can help change that. If you're of a mind to add your weight, log on to www.spiritofireland.org to add your support and send your thoughts to our politicians by using the *Energise* database in Appendix II. Even if you remain deeply sceptical of the Spirit of Ireland plan or Fine Gael's ability to deliver NewERA exclusively through state companies, you should consider contacting our political leaders to add your voice to the concerns about Ireland's exposure and complacency about peak. At the very least, the Irish government needs to transfer the grid to EirGrid, commence the building of the new 440kW and 220kW lines, discuss interconnection with the French government, accelerate green energy development and prepare Ireland for energy shortages from peak oil.

You're just finishing *Energise*. What you've learned, I've learned, and hopefully you'll log on to my website, www.eddiehobbs.com, for ongoing updates and investments you can explore. The appendices also contain a list of key references: websites, prolific and highly informed writers and key reports if you wish to delve even further. I hope that you will see the clear logic to investing in energy, commodities and energy efficiency and take personal action, but you can also do something more important. We are in a race, whether we like it or not. The Age of Scarcity has begun.

Ireland can become much more energy savvy, but its political leaders lead from behind, and they first need people to prod them in the right direction. Many Irish people will read this book, perhaps for the first time understanding the nature of the peril we face. Tens of thousands more can be reached by widening the discussion. You can add to the viral effect simply by talking to friends, neighbours and work colleagues about the issues *Energise* has raised for you and your family, adding to debate and to the controversy about Ireland's extreme addiction to oil and gas.

At first it won't be easy; it never is when you become a lightning rod. Reactions will range from disbelief to pillory, as all the myths about oil are dredged up in defence of the status quo, because it's easier to keep things just as they are, that's human nature. You'll be told to shut up about oil; that you've become a Cassandra and, anyway, prices are falling again.

But point to your new investments, tune people into the oil-price spikes as they pull and push economic reversal and growth, and tell them about the energy-efficiency revolution. In time, they'll come round, especially when you stress the positive outcomes that change will bring.

I wish you well with your own endeavours over the years ahead and, who knows, we might meet some day on an Irish beach having travelled there in our electric cars powered by Irish green electricity – otherwise we'll meet on the way to the local mart, you on your bicycle and me on Ned the donkey.

Thanks for reading *Energise*.

Eddie.

Appendix I. Technical stuff – analysing PLCs

Common sense can get you pretty far in picking good energy-biased investments, especially if you delegate stock picking to specialist fund managers or if you invest in exchange-traded funds (ETFs). These require you to make the asset allocation decision yourself and let the fund do the rest, whether the stock picking is done by human intelligence, as it is in actively managed funds, or by market capitalisation, as it is with many ETFs.

However, when you stray into the world of picking stocks yourself, it's wise to acquaint yourself with some of the basic tools for analysing the financial information produced by PLCs, even if your stockbroker does much of the work by feeding you analysts' papers and commentary. It's especially important to do this when you stray under the radar screen of big PLCs into the smaller companies not covered by analysts. To help with this I've explained below some of the basic formulae and language used in the energy sector.

Finally, if you want to avoid the high commission costs of domestic stockbrokers try TD Waterhouse, an online and UK-based trading platform from one of the world's largest discount brokers, the Toronto-Dominion Bank Financial Group. TD Waterhouse charges flat-rate fees per trade, which can be as low as £9.95, and it covers ETFs and stocks across sixteen international stock markets.

Energy language

The word 'energy' comes from two Greek words, **en** (in) and **ergon** (work) and energy itself is measured in **joules**. However, to understand the basic energy formula, it's best to start with Sir Isaac Newton's definition of **force**. A newton (n) is the amount of force that accelerates a mass of 1 kilogram (kg) at a rate of 1 metre per second per second (ms^{-2}), so the formula becomes:

Force (n) = **Mass** (kg) × **Acceleration** (ms^{-2})

When a force moves something, it supplies energy, and energy is measured in **joules** (j). One joule is defined as the amount of energy supplied when a force of 1 newton causes a movement of 1 metre and so the formula is:

Energy (joules) = **Force** (newtons) × **Distance** (in metres)

Power is the rate at which energy is converted from one form to another, or is transferred from one place to another, and it is measured in **watts** (W), where 1 watt is defined as 1 joule per second.

Under the **First Law of Thermodynamics**, energy is always conserved, so, in any process, the total amount of energy remains unchanged. When you switch on a 60-watt light bulb, for example, you convert 60 joules of energy each second into light and waste heat in an inefficient ratio of 5% (light) and 95% (heat), in the case of the conventional tungsten-filament light bulb. However, in practice, it is more common to measure energy by the amount of power used over a given time period. So, for example, if the power of an air-conditioning unit is 3kW and it runs for two hours, we say it has consumed 6 kilowatt-hours (kWh).

A kilowatt is 1,000 watts. Larger measurements of energy, for example by power plants or by a nation, require different prefixes. A million watts (i.e. 10 × 10 × 10 × 10 × 10 × 10, or 10^6 watts) make a megawatt (MW), a billion make a gigawatt (GW) and a trillion a terawatt (TW). Other prefixes are used to describe tiny units of energy created. Here are those you are most likely to encounter:

Exa-	E	10^{18}	one quintillion
Peta-	P	10^{15}	one quadrillion
Tera-	T	10^{12}	one trillion
Giga-	G	10^9	one billion
Mega-	M	10^6	one million
Kilo-	K	10^3	one thousand
Hecto-	H	10^2	one hundred
Deca-	da	10	ten
Deci-	D	10^{-1}	one-tenth
Centi-	C	10^{-2}	one-hundredth
Milli-	M	10^{-3}	one-thousandth
Micro-	μ	10^{-6}	one-millionth
Nano-	N	10^{-9}	one-billionth

When energy is converted from one form to another, its efficiency is measured by comparing output energy with input energy. In photovoltaic (PV) cells, and despite technological advances, efficiency is in the low range (10% to 20%); in hydropower, efficiency can be as high as 90%. The 'lost' energy is not actually lost, but instead is typically transformed by the mechanical or electrical devices used in the process into wasted heat.

National and global energy consumption is frequently reported in the quantities of fuel used of various types: barrels of oil, tons of coal, cubic feet of gas and so on. These, however, can be combined into a common measurement, **megatonnes of oil equivalent (Mtoe)**, where 1 Mtoe is equal to 41.9Pj (Petajoules).

Energy can be measured at different levels. The energy released when a fossil fuel is burned in a power station is known as **primary energy**, but due to transmission losses, for example in the electricity grid (where energy can be transformed into heat), the **delivered energy** will be lower. Further loss or leakage of energy takes place in the conversion of electricity that a household receives, so **useful energy** will be lower than delivered energy. Much energy is lost due to household inefficiencies, such as electrical appliances being left switched on in stand-by mode or simply because a hot tap is left running.

The paperwork you'll read from PLCs

Publicly quoted companies produce half-yearly accounts for the London stock market and quarterly accounts for the US stock markets. The accounts produced are the **profit-and-loss account**, the **balance sheet** and the **cash-flow statement**. These operate under a set of accounting standards and are produced by **independent auditors**. Publicly quoted companies are required to produce considerably more information than companies not publicly quoted, including a **directors' report**, together with detailed **notes to the accounts**.

The accounts usually open with a statement from the **chairperson**, but the most important statement is the **auditors' report**. It is the job of the auditors to certify that the accounts represent **a true and fair view** of the company's profits. Where the accounts are **qualified** (i.e. criticised) by an auditor, the position is damaging for a publicly quoted company.

The profit-and-loss account shows the trading results over the past financial period, measuring it against similar results for the previous financial period. The cash-flow statement is simply another angle from which the same figures can be examined. Many businesses can look robust in their profit-and-loss accounts and balance sheets, but may have messed up their cash flows. **Over time, what a company reports in profits should be reflected in the cash flow generated**.

A typical balance sheet is shown in table A.1. It gives a snapshot, at a particular point in time, of the total value of the company's assets and liabilities. Equivalent figures are provided in balance sheets for the previous financial period. The balance sheet is a

Table A.1 Example profit-and-loss account

Bandon Biofuel PLC – Profit-and-loss account, 2008

	€000	
Revenue	100,000	**Gross profit margin**
Cost of Sales	48,000	$52,000/100,000 = 52\%$
Gross profit	52,000	
Operating expenses		
Selling & admin.	20,000	
Research & development	10,000	**Net profit margin**
	30,000	$14,700/100,000 = 14.7\%$
Income from operations	22,000	
Investment income	500	
Income before tax	22,500	
Tax	7,800	
Net income	14,700	
Earnings per share	2.94	**Earnings per share**
Shares outstanding	5,000	$14,700/5,000 = €2.94$

useful measure to provide an overview of the wealth of a company, but, taken in isolation, it can be misleading. Some companies manipulate their financial data – a practice quite within the rules of accounting standards – by methods such as bringing forward some items and delaying others in order to present the balance sheet in a better light. This is called **window–dressing**. The term '**creative accounting**' is used when figures are skewed excessively, as witnessed for WorldCom, whose ex-CEO Bernie Ebbers was sentenced to twenty-five years in prison after being found guilty of accounting fraud. Several balance sheets may be produced by a business, but large companies usually have a holding company that produces the **consolidated balance sheet** for all of its subsidiary companies, each of which will have separate balance sheets.

A study of the information produced by companies can give you helpful insights. An investor's objective is to discover if the price quoted for the shares is too high or too low on the basis of the information presented in the accounts. Where careful analysis leads to an opinion that the share price is low, this represents an opportunity to buy. On the other hand, where analysis reveals that the share price is too high, this may be an opportunity to go short. Most of the information you need to examine converts to **ratios**. Ratios arise when you compare one number against another.

Bandon Biofuel PLC is a very simple company – all of its figures have come in with nice round sums. Bandon Biofuel doesn't exist. Nevertheless, its fictional profit-and-loss account and balance sheet (Table A.2) should help you to understand where these ratios arise and how to calculate them. There is also a statement of cash flows for another fictitious company, Wicklow Windmills PLC (Table A.3), so you can see what one looks like and what to look for in it.

Table A.2 Example balance sheet

Bandon Biofuel PLC – Balance sheet, 2008

	€000
Current assets	
Cash & cash equivalents	43,000
Accounts receivable	60,000
Stock	41,000
Prepayments	2,000
	146,000
Fixed assets	
Property & equipment	20,000
Depreciation	(2,000)
	18,000
	164,000
Current liabilities	
Accounts payable	12,000
Accruals	37,000
	49,000
Long-term debt	3,000
	52,000
Shareholders' equity	
Ordinary shares: €1 par value	5,000
Additional paid in capital	40,000
Retained earnings	67,000
	112,000
Total liabilities & shareholders' equity	164,000

Current ratio
$146,000/49,000 = 2.98$

Cash per share
$43,000/5,000 = €8.60$

Debt/equity ratio
$3000/112,000 = 2.7$

Table A.3 Example cash-flow statement

Wicklow Windmills PLC– Statement of cash flows		
	€000 2007	€000 2008
Cash flows from operating activities: Net income	15,000	16,000
Adjustment for depreciation: Depreciation	1,800	2,000
Changes in operating assets & liabilities: Accounts receivable	(18,000)	(12,000)
Stock	(12,000)	(8,000)
Accounts payable	2,000	4,000
Accrued expenses	3,000	6,000
Net cash from operating expenses	(8,200)	8,000

Earnings per share

The profit-and-loss account tells you how much **net income** the
company has earned over a particular time period. This net income
has been earned by the shareholders. How much is attributed to
each shareholder depends on the total number of shares outstanding. In the example, Bandon Biofuel's net income was €14.7 million, with 5 million shares outstanding. The earnings per share
(EPS) is calculated by dividing the net income by the total number
of shares outstanding, giving Bandon Biofuel an EPS of €2.94.

P/E ratio

The P/E ratio is the market's price tag for a share and is calculated
by dividing the current share price by the earnings per share over
the past twelve months. The P/E ratio is often quoted next to a
stock in newspaper listings. Let's say that Bandon Biofuel is currently trading at €44.10 per share. The P/E ratio is the share price

(€44.10) divided by the EPS (€2.94), which equals 15. Therefore its stock is said to be trading at 15 times earnings.

You need to be a little bit careful of P/E ratios because EPS may be based on past earnings, in which case the P/E ratio is called a **trailing** P/E ratio. Technical analysts investigate the potential future value of a company and often use the **projected** earnings per share. This means that the current share price is divided by the projected EPS, in which case the result is a **forward** P/E ratio.

Net assets per share

Net assets per share (NAV) is calculated by dividing the ordinary shareholders' funds by the number of ordinary shares outstanding. For Bandon Biofuel, the shareholders' funds appear on the balance sheet at €112 million, which is divided by the 5 million shares in existence, giving a NAV of €22.40.

Gross margin and net margin

The gross margin and net margin in the profit-and-loss account are probably the terms most familiar to those involved in retailing. The **gross margin** is calculated by dividing gross profit by total sales. This is an indication of how much profit is being made at point of sale, which can be ploughed back into the business to pay for its operating costs and expenses. It does not tell us how much of every euro made at point of sale adds to the bottom line. To calculate Bandon Biofuel's gross margin, you divide the gross profit of €52 million by total sales of €100 million, which gives a gross profit margin of 52%.

In its profit-and-loss account, the bottom line is the net income after paying operating expenses and tax. This is €14.7 million, producing a **net margin**, when compared to sales of 14.7%.

The important thing about gross profit margin and net profit margin, just like many other ratios, is how they compare to previous figures.

For the sake of clarity, the simplified accounts for Bandon Biofuel do not contain the equivalent figures for the previous financial period. In the real world, you will be presented with these figures. If you examine the gross profit margin and the net profit margin for the current and past financial years, you will be able to see whether or not margins are being maintained. If they are not, this gives you cause for further investigation.

Dividend ratios

The dividend yield, which acts as an indicator of the current cost of a share relative to the income it produces, is calculated by dividing the gross dividend per share by the share price. Let's say that Bandon Biofuel's shares are trading at €40 and that the directors have decided to pay a dividend of €1.50 per share. This means the yield will be €1.50 divided by €40, producing a dividend yield of 3.75%. Now, let's say a few weeks later the share price has jumped dramatically to €50. Remember, the dividend is still €1.50 per share. The new dividend yield will therefore be lower: €1.50 divided by €50 equals 3.0%. Falling dividend yields normally means increasing share prices, and vice versa.

Dividend cover is another way of expressing the proportion of profit that the directors decide to pay out as the dividend. For Bandon Biofuel, the total profit for 2008 is €14.7 million. The directors have decided to pay €1.50 per share to the 5 million shareholders, so that will cost the company €7.5 million. The dividend cover is calculated by dividing the profit by the total cost of paying the dividends: in this case, €14.7 million divided by €7.5 million. Bandon Biofuel is therefore said to have dividend cover of 1.96 times.

The dividend cover is a measure of the **safety** of the dividend. The more strongly covered it is, the safer it is and the lower the chance of the company reducing it or dropping it entirely should profits fall. When companies pay dividends, even though they have just made a loss, they do so out of their **reserves**.

The **dividend per share** (DPS) is the total amount of money the directors are setting aside to pay dividends divided by the total number of shares – the reverse of the earlier calculation. In our example the directors are setting aside €7.5 million and there are 5 million shares, so the DPS is €1.50.

The **dividend payout ratio** measures how much of the company's profits are being paid out in dividends. It is calculated by dividing the dividend per share by the earnings per share. The bigger and stronger a company is, the more likely it is that the dividend payout ratio will head towards 50% – meaning that 50% of profits are being paid out as dividends. Where the dividend payout ratio is particularly high, this can be a sign that the **dividend may be cut**.

Bear in mind the impact of **tax** on dividends. Companies paying dividends are often compelled to retain tax, normally at the basic rate for taxpayers, and to pay it to the Revenue. The dividend will be paid **net** and will therefore be known as a **net dividend**. To calculate the gross dividend, you will need to gross up the net figure by reference to the basic rate of tax. For example, let's say a net dividend is quoted at €1.40 per share and the basic rate of tax is 20%. This means that €1.40 represents 80% of a higher figure. To arrive at that higher figure, divide €1.40 by 80 and multiply by 100. Here, the gross dividend is €1.75 per share.

Dividend yields, particularly those of the strong stocks used by investors for income purposes, are often compared to **bond yields**. The most common position is to find that equity yields less than bond yields; this is the natural position for the market. A bond investor will not gain increased income, but an equity investor is looking not just for an increase in the capital value of the share but also for an increase in dividend payments to be decided by the directors of the company. It is for this reason that dividend yields are usually lower than bond yields and are said to be trading at a **discount** to bond yields.

Gearing

Gearing, or **leveraging**, is a term used to describe the relationship between money borrowed (i.e. debt) and shareholders' money (i.e. equity). In much the same way as gearing is used to maximise return on property investments, companies use gearing to fuel growth. The level of gearing, or the relationship between debt and equity, is also called the **debt/equity ratio**.

The more debt a company holds, the more it is exposed to interest-rate risk. When interest rates rise, the company's ability to service its debt can begin to affect its business. This does not affect **equity finance**, however, which is also called **risk capital**. A highly geared, or highly leveraged, company is one that has a large amount of money borrowed in relation to its equity, while a low leveraged company is one that has large equity and little borrowings. The **debt/equity ratio** is calculated by dividing long-term debt by the total level of shareholders' equity.

The current ratio

The current ratio, or **liquid ratio**, measures the short-term liquidity of a company by comparing its current assets (i.e. cash, stocks/inventories, receivables, etc.) against its current liabilities, such as accounts payable, accruals, etc. It is calculated by dividing current assets by current liabilities. As a general rule of thumb, investors look for a relationship between current assets and current liabilities of, at the very least, 2:1.

Return on equity

Return on equity (ROE) is a commonly used measure of profitability. It is calculated by dividing the company's earnings by the total shareholders' equity. In the case of Bandon Biofuel, this means dividing €14.7 million (the net income from the profit-and-loss account) by the total shareholders' equity (taken from the balance sheet). The calculation is €14.7 million earnings divided by €112 million equity. This gives 13.13% ROE. For large companies, a ROE in excess of 15% is regarded as excellent. For smaller companies ROEs in excess of 20% are typically demanded by investors in order to compensate them for taking the additional risk of not investing in larger companies.

Return on assets

Return on assets (ROA) is another commonly used ratio and it measures the pre-tax profits of the company as compared to the capital used to run the business. It can sometimes be more useful than ROE, which tells how the company's earnings relate to the shareholders' money, because ROE tells how profitable a company is, irrespective of financing, and ignores the benefits of a low tax rate. Instead, ROA measures the return against all monies, including loans. To arrive at ROA, take the profit before tax and before interest on long-term debt and divide it by the assets employed. The assets employed will be the shareholders' funds, but not including goodwill, long-term loans, deferred tax and majority shareholder interests, all of which will be noted on the balance sheet.

Other terms you may come across

Scrip dividends: An opportunity to take more shares in lieu of a dividend payment.

Fixed charge: When this appears in connection with borrowing it indicates that specific assets have been **pledged against the borrowing**. This is to differentiate it from a **floating charge** where **all** of the assets of the business are assigned against the borrowing.

Unsecured creditors: Those transacting business with the company whose lending to the company has not been secured. Typically, this means suppliers, who are the last in the queue when a company goes bust. The local tax authorities are also unsecured creditors, but may be given the first position in the unsecured creditors' queue.

Overtrading: Refers to a company that may be growing too fast in comparison to the resources it has to keep the business going.

Rights issue: Refers to a decision by a company to sell more shares as a way of raising capital. This usually depresses share prices because it increases the number of shares in circulation.

Goodwill: Often appears in balance sheets and is regarded as an **intangible asset**. It will have its own note in the accounts to tell you how it has been calculated. When a company is taken over, the difference between the acquisition price paid and the net assets of the company is regarded as the premium the buyer pays for the goodwill of the business.

Contingent liabilities: Appears where there is, for example, a legal case pending against a company that it could lose and it is entered in the balance sheet as a possible liability that it may need to pay.

Warrants: These are a way for a company to raise money that does not appear in its balance sheet. Warrant is another name for guarantee. Warrants issued by companies give the holder the right to subscribe, at a certain, fixed price, to the shares of the company at a future date. Generally, the subscription price will be fixed above the current share price of the shares.

Revaluation reserves: These occur when a company revalues some of its assets and finds that they are worth more than had previously been noted in the accounts. This typically happens in relation to property.

Net tangible asset value: The net asset value, excluding goodwill.

Ex-dividend: When you buy a share ex-dividend, it means you are not entitled to the current dividend payment. That will go to the selling shareholder.

Cum-dividend: This is the opposite to ex-dividend and means that when you buy the share you will get the payment of the current dividend.

Getting organised

Make sure you use **specialist software** that allows you to track the values of the various shares you have and the decisions that you take. **Quicken** is a good example of a workable piece of software. If you want to be very active, you need to bear in mind that trading costs money, so locate a good **discount stockbroker** that gives good value for money and doesn't overcharge for small trades.

Get your thinking right

Rule number one: be prepared to invest for the **long term**. Speculators go into equity markets telling themselves that they are in it for the long term, but in reality they are hoping to make a short-term killing and they jump out at the first sign of trouble. The worst thing you can do is to make the typical herd mistake of buying in at the top and selling out at the bottom. You should buy stocks systematically, **spreading** your investments **over time**. This reduces the risk of loading all of your bets into a very short period, which is inadvisable even in a strong bull market in a sector like energy and commodities.

You wouldn't go to a house auction without a set price in your mind and stocks are no different. After doing your research, *set a price* at which you will buy a particular stock and stick to it. Having put all of the necessary effort into researching a company, don't stop after you have bought the stock. Stay on top of it and examine all of the financial information produced by the company. Don't be reluctant to ring the company secretary to get accounts and to ask for further information. That's what the company secretary and his or her office is there for, i.e. to look after shareholders and prospective shareholders. Remember, their job is to serve you.

Finally, **measure your performance** against an appropriate stock market index rather than against how others are doing with their stock portfolios. Your stock portfolio will directly reflect your personality and your research.

The market movers and shakers

Market-makers have to do just that: make a market. They are compelled to deal in certain types of share. **Broker dealers**, on the other hand, may hold shares on their own books, which they will then sell to clients, but they have no obligation to make the market. Market-makers and broker dealers may also act as **agency brokers**, executing clients' buy and sell orders and charging a commission on each deal.

Investors can buy shares for cash or **on the margin**, which means using borrowed funds. These funds will be lent by the broker, who will charge interest on the loan. The **broker's loan rate** is usually about 1% above the prime rate. If you are playing with borrowed money you can **magnify your return**, but equally you can **magnify your losses**. By using this service, you buy shares and delay payment for them, selling them later at a higher price and clearing the loan. Things can go disastrously wrong, however. If your stock value halves overnight, you may be subject to a **margin call**. This means that you must put up additional collateral to cover your loan or your broker will sell your stock immediately.

Contracts for difference (CFDs) are a derivative product that enable investors to buy exposure but not ownership of a large number of shares for a small amount down. A cover call on CFDs after a stock market fall is about the most unwelcome phone call you'll ever receive, requiring you to buy the full exposure to the stocks in cash. Borrowing money or using derivatives like CFDs to invest in stocks is unwise, unless you have the resources to cover the downside risk that leveraging brings.

Shorting is achieved using the margin account. It is not for the fainthearted or the inexperienced. This does not automatically mean that shorting is not for you. If the sums of money involved do not represent a large proportion of your overall financial strength, it can make sense. But in the hands of the uninformed, borrowing heavily to invest in equities is simply a form of gambling.

Routes to investment

Dealing with stockbrokers

As a direct investor, you may wish to make your investments via a stockbroker, whom you can then call on for help or advice, as necessary. If this option appeals to you, here's the lowdown on engaging your very own broker.

In Ireland, stockbrokers tend to be expensive. This is especially so for the active trader, who is likely to find better value from online discount international specialists, like TD Waterhouse, who charge low, flat-rate fees per trade. The level of commission charged by local stockbrokers scale down depending on the deal size, but you can expect commissions to begin at 1.5% to 2%. Government stamp duty of 1% is also payable. Remember, when shares are sold, a similar commission is charged again.

When you give a stockbroker the discretion to actively trade your portfolio, bear in mind the inherent conflict between trading and boosting commission revenues. You should also insist on measuring the return on your portfolio against the index of the market in which the stockbroker has placed your money because you can bypass active trading costs simply by buying exchange-traded funds of the type highlighted in *Energise*.

Your shares can be held in paper form, as certificates, or electronically. When you hold your share certificates you can deal through any stockbroker – you remain the legal owner at all times and your dividends are paid directly to you. The downside is that you can't move as quickly as electronic settling.

Your shares can be held electronically in two ways. The first is through a Crest Personal Member account, which registers you as the owner of the shares and the direct recipient of dividends and gives you the freedom to shop the market for best dealing rates and flat fees among stockbrokers who maintain the service for you. The second way is through a Crest Nominee account, which differs fundamentally because you are not the legal owner of the shares, although you remain the beneficial owner of them. In this case, in the event of the liquidation of the stockbroker, your investment might be at risk to the liquidator. There is already legal precedent in Ireland where the courts ruled in favour of the liquidator after the collapse of a Cork stockbroker, marking a fundamental shift in default risk for investors who use nominee services. The stockbroker establishes a nominee company to hold client shares in a single account. You pay flat fees to the stockbroker for maintaining the account, typically up to €100 per year, and you execute all deals through the stockbroker's service and prices.

Discount broking

Modern telecommunications have revolutionised the service available to individual private investors. The **internet** gives investors access to information that was previously the exclusive preserve of stockbrokers. Before the introduction of the internet, investors had to pay fat fees to brokers to cover the expense involved in communicating with somebody down on the stock exchange floor, who was following your buying and selling instructions. Changes in technology have now shifted power down line to the small investor, reducing trading costs dramatically. More developments are on the way including new platforms that facilitate trading across a wide variety of exchanges.

Following the abolition of fixed commission agreements between stockbroker firms many moons ago, a new generation of stockbrokers has emerged. For the small independent investor, the most valuable of these is the **discount broker**. Discount brokers do not get involved in bringing a company to market, an activity known as an **initial public offering (IPO)**, and may not have research analysts on staff. Normally, the only thing that a discount brokerage does is to execute orders for buying and selling. It does not offer advice.

Discount brokers can be split into two categories: ordinary discount brokers, who will carry out instructions, but may also provide some research material, news, etc., and deep discount brokers, who do not usually provide ancillary services and merely execute instructions.

Building up a relationship with a good discount broker is particularly important if you fancy yourself as an active trader. Full-service brokers charge transaction fees, typically up to 1.5% of a small investment, with a scaled-down percentage for higher sums. Remember, there is commission at both ends – when you buy and when you sell. Full-service stockbrokers are valuable to investors who'd like access to research and analysts before undertaking trades and they have an important role to play in markets.

Under the rules of the European Union's Markets in Financial Instruments Directive (MIFID), a full-service broker is required to undertake a detailed fact-find of your position and to know exactly what your targets are. They will usually provide you with a wealth of research material and will develop attractive portfolio models to convince you that you should invest in the stocks the full-service brokerage believes are best for you. Remember, most stockbrokers, especially in Ireland, haven't yet cottoned on to the depletion of natural resources. They still see it as a theme and not a fundamental economic switch, one that should utterly change conventional portfolio construction, so don't be surprised by recommendations from them to invest in airlines and other sectors at high risk to energy-led inflation.

Giving instructions to your broker

There are different types of instructions or orders you can give your stockbroker.

LIMIT ORDER

When you give your broker a limit order, you are telling your broker to buy or sell a particular stock at a specific price, or better. For example, if a stock is trading in London at £7 and you want to buy it at £6.50, you can place a **purchase limit** at £6.50. It also works in reverse, which is when you are selling a stock. For example, if you are holding a stock at €15 per share and you fancy that if it goes to €20 per share you will sell, you can place this **selling limit** with your broker.

DAY ORDER

This is an instruction to your broker to buy or sell a stock at a particular price on a particular day. If the transaction cannot be placed on that particular day, your order does not carry forward.

STOP ORDER

A stop order is used to protect the profit you have gained, or to limit any further losses. The most frequently used is the **stop-loss order**, which tells your broker to sell if the stock hits a specific price. For example, say you bought a stock at €20 and it's now trading at €40. You may wish to protect your gain by placing a stop-loss order at €35. When prices fall, it's not always very neat, and the nearest market price the broker may be able to get for you could be less than the €35 limit you stipulated. For example, the broker may be only able to do the trade at €33.

Stop orders can also work in reverse, particularly when you are selling short. This is where you provide an instruction to your broker to buy up a share if it falls to a specific price, set by you.

GOOD-THIS-MONTH ORDER

Where you provide an order to your broker to buy or to sell a stock at a particular price during a long time period, such as a month, this is known as a **good-this-month order** (GTM).

GOOD-THIS-WEEK ORDER

The same thing can be done for a week-long period, in which case it is known as a **good-this-week order** (GTW).

GOOD-TILL-CANCELLED ORDER

Where you give an open-ended instruction to your broker to buy or sell a particular stock when it hits a specific price, this is called a **good-till-cancelled order** (GTC). The GTC remains an **open order** until such time as you cancel it.

Investing in small companies

It's only common sense to invest in large-capitalisation, sector-dominant mature companies like Petrobras, BHP Billiton and the Potash Corporation of Saskatchewan and mid-sized companies that dominate new sectors like wind and solar, but in your travels you'll come across oodles of new, small companies in existing and embryonic sectors not yet on the radar screen for institutional investors because they're too small and illiquid. These can provide explosive growth if you can learn the trick of weeding out losers and focusing on small, strong, well-managed companies with breakthrough products, patents or inventions.

Small stocks can grow more quickly than large stocks. Because of the link between earnings and share price, rapidly growing profits can impact the share price of a small company very quickly. Small stocks have an awful lot more room to breathe and, unlike large stocks, are usually in less restrictive and competitive markets. This means their earnings can grow a lot faster until, of course, they, in turn, become very large companies and are affected by the same factors as large stocks.

Investment in small stocks will be successful only if you undertake careful, planned and systematic research. If you do not have the time to invest in undertaking the work necessary, stay out of this market. It cannot be done well 'on the hoof'. Recommended reading for small investors is *The Motley Fool* by the Gardner brothers, who are themselves active traders and who outline their system for managing small stocks in their book.

Appendix II. How to contact all the members of the Dáil

The postal address for all TDs and senators is: Oireachtas Éireann, Leinster House, Kildare Street, Dublin 2.

Remember, when writing to a TD or a senator at Leinster House, postage is free; you don't need to put a stamp on the envelope.

Alternatively, you can email your TD or a senator, or all TDs and senators, using the email contact details listed below. (Party key: CC: Ceann Comhairle; FF: Fianna Fáil; FG: Fine Gael; G: Green Party; I: Independent; L: Labour Party; PD: Progressive Democrats; SF: Sinn Féin.)

TD name	Constituency	Email
Mr Bobby Aylward (FF)	Carlow-Kilkenny	bobby.aylward@oireachtas.ie
Mr Phil Hogan (FG)	Carlow-Kilkenny	philip.hogan@oireachtas.ie
Mr John McGuinness (FF)	Carlow-Kilkenny	john.mcguinness@oireachtas.ie
Mr M. J. Nolan (FF)	Carlow-Kilkenny	mj.nolan@oireachtas.ie
Ms Mary Alexandra White (G)	Carlow-Kilkenny	marya.white@oireachtas.ie
Ms Margaret Conlon (FF)	Cavan-Monaghan	margaret.conlon@oireachtas.ie
Mr Seymour Crawford (FG)	Cavan-Monaghan	seymour.crawford@oireachtas.ie
Mr Caoimhghín Ó Caoláin (SF)	Cavan-Monaghan	ocaolain@oireachtas.ie
Dr Rory O'Hanlon (FF)	Cavan-Monaghan	rory.ohanlon@oireachtas.ie
Mr Brendan Smith (FF)	Cavan-Monaghan	minister@agriculture.gov.ie
Mr Pat Breen (FG)	Clare	pat.breen@oireachtas.ie
Mr Joe Carey (FG)	Clare	joe.carey@oireachtas.ie
Mr Timmy Dooley (FF)	Clare	timmy.dooley@oireachtas.ie
Mr Tony Killeen (FF)	Clare	tony.killeen@oireachtas.ie

Mr Michael Ahern (FF)	Cork East	michael.ahern@oireachtas.ie
Mr Edward O'Keeffe (FF)	Cork East	ned.okeeffe@oireachtas.ie
Mr Sean Sherlock (L)	Cork East	sean.sherlock@oireachtas.ie
Mr David Stanton (FG)	Cork East	david.stanton@oireachtas.ie
Mr Bernard Allen (FG)	Cork North-Central	bernard.allen@oireachtas.ie
Mr Billy Kelleher (FF)	Cork North-Central	billykelleher@eircom.net
Ms Kathleen Lynch (L)	Cork North-Central	kathleen.lynch@oireachtas.ie
Mr Noel O'Flynn (FF)	Cork North-Central	noel.oflynn@oireachtas.ie
Mr Michael Creed (FG)	Cork North-West	michael.creed@oireachtas.ie
Mr Michael Moynihan (FF)	Cork North-West	michael.moynihan.td@oireachtas.ie
Mr Batt O'Keeffe (FF)	Cork North-West	minister_okeeffe@education.gov.ie
Ms Deirdre Clune (FG)	Cork South-Central	deirdre.clune@oireachtas.ie
Mr Simon Coveney (FG)	Cork South-Central	simon.coveney@oireachtas.ie
Mr Ciarán Lynch (L)	Cork South-Central	ciaran.lynch@oireachtas.ie
Mr Micheál Martin (FF)	Cork South-Central	minister@dfa.ie
Mr Michael McGrath (FF)	Cork South-Central	michael.mcgrath@oireachtas.ie
Mr Jim O'Keeffe (FG)	Cork South-West	jim.okeeffe@oireachtas.ie
Mr Christy O'Sullivan (FF)	Cork South-West	christy.osullivan@oireachtas.ie
Mr P. J. Sheehan (FG)	Cork South-West	pj.sheehan@oireachtas.ie
Mr Niall Blaney (FF)	Donegal North-East	niall.blaney@oireachtas.ie
Dr James McDaid (FF)	Donegal North-East	jim.mcdaid@oireachtas.ie
Mr Joe McHugh (FG)	Donegal North-East	joe.mchugh@oireachtas.ie
Ms Mary Coughlan (FF)	Donegal South-West	tanaiste@entemp.ie
Mr Dinny McGinley (FG)	Donegal South-West	dinny.mcginley@oireachtas.ie
Mr Bertie Ahern (FF)	Dublin Central	bertie.ahern@oireachtas.ie
Mr Cyprian Brady (FF)	Dublin Central	cyprian.brady@oireachtas.ie
Mr Joe Costello (L)	Dublin Central	joe.costello@oireachtas.ie
Ms Maureen O'Sullivan (I)	Dublin Central	maureen.osullivan@oireachtas.ie
Mr John Curran (FF)	Dublin Mid-West	john.curran@oireachtas.ie
Mr Paul Nicholas Gogarty (G)	Dublin Mid-West	paul.gogarty@oireachtas.ie

Ms Mary Harney (PD)	Dublin Mid-West	minister's_office@health.irlgov.ie
Ms Joanna Tuffy (L)	Dublin Mid-West	joanna.tuffy@oireachtas.ie
Mr Brendan Kenneally (FF)	Dublin North	bwk@eircom.net
Mr Darragh O'Brien (FF)	Dublin North	darragh.obrien@oireachtas.ie
Dr James Reilly (FG)	Dublin North	james.reilly@oireachtas.ie
Mr Trevor Sargent (G)	Dublin North	trevor.sargent@oireachtas.ie
Mr Richard Bruton (FG)	Dublin North-Central	richard.bruton@oireachtas.ie
Mr Sean Haughey (FF)	Dublin North-Central	sean_haughey@education.gov.ie
Mr Finian McGrath (I)	Dublin North-Central	finian.mcgrath@oireachtas.ie
Mr Tommy Broughan (L)	Dublin North-East	thomas.p.broughan@oireachtas.ie
Mr Terence Flanagan (FG)	Dublin North-East	terence.flanagan@oireachtas.ie
Dr Michael J. Woods (FF)	Dublin North-East	michael.woods@oireachtas.ie
Mr Noel Ahern (FF)	Dublin North-West	noel.ahern@oireachtas.ie
Mr Pat Carey (FF)	Dublin North-West	minister.carey@taoiseach.gov.ie
Ms Róisín Shortall (L)	Dublin North-West	roisin.shortall@oireachtas.ie
Mr Tom Kitt (FF)	Dublin South	tom.kitt@oireachtas.ie
Ms Olivia Mitchell (FG)	Dublin South	olivia.mitchell@oireachtas.ie
Mr Eamon Ryan (G)	Dublin South	minister.ryan@dcmnr.gov.ie
Mr Alan Shatter (FG)	Dublin South	alan.shatter@oireachtas.ie
Mr Seán Ardagh (FF)	Dublin South-Central	sean@ardagh.org
Ms Catherine Byrne (FG)	Dublin South-Central	catherine.byrne@oireachtas.ie
Mr Michael Mulcahy (FF)	Dublin South-Central	michael.mulcahy@oireachtas.ie
Mr Aengus Ó Snodaigh (SF)	Dublin South-Central	aengus.osnodaigh@oireachtas.ie
Dr Mary Upton (L)	Dublin South-Central	mary.upton@oireachtas.ie
Mr Chris Andrews (FF)	Dublin South-East	chris.andrews@oireachtas.ie
Ms Lucinda Creighton (FG)	Dublin South-East	lucinda.creighton@oireachtas.ie
Mr John Gormley (G)	Dublin South-East	minister@environ.ie
Mr Ruairí Quinn (L)	Dublin South-East	ruairi.quinn@oireachtas.ie
Mr Brian Hayes (FG)	Dublin South-West	brian.hayes@oireachtas.ie
Mr Conor Lenihan (FF)	Dublin South-West	conor.lenihan@oireachtas.ie

Mr Charlie O'Connor (FF)	Dublin South-West	charlie.oconnor@oireachtas.ie
Mr Pat Rabbitte (L)	Dublin South-West	pat.rabbitte@oireachtas.ie
Ms Joan Burton (L)	Dublin West	joan.burton@oireachtas.ie
Mr Brian Joseph Lenihan (FF)	Dublin West	minister@finance.gov.ie
Mr Leo Varadkar (FG)	Dublin West	leo.varadkar@oireachtas.ie
Mr Barry Andrews (FF)	Dún Laoghaire	barry.andrews@oireachtas.ie
Mr Sean Barrett (FG)	Dún Laoghaire	sean.barrett@oireachtas.ie
Mr Ciaran Cuffe (G)	Dún Laoghaire	ciaran.cuffe@oireachtas.ie
Mr Eamon Gilmore (L)	Dún Laoghaire	eamon.gilmore@oireachtas.ie
Ms Mary Hanafin (FF)	Dún Laoghaire	minister@welfare.ie
Mr Ulick Burke (FG)	Galway East	ulick.burke@oireachtas.ie
Mr Paul Connaughton (FG)	Galway East	paul.connaughton@oireachtas.ie
Mr Michael P. Kitt (FF)	Galway East	michael.kitt@oireachtas.ie
Mr Noel Treacy (FF)	Galway East	noel.treacy@oireachtas.ie
Mr Frank Fahey (FF)	Galway West	frank.fahey@oireachtas.ie
Mr Noel Grealish (PD)	Galway West	noel.grealish@oireachtas.ie
Mr Michael D. Higgins (L)	Galway West	michael.higgins@oireachtas.ie
Mr Pádraic McCormack (FG)	Galway West	padraic.mccormack@oireachtas.ie
Mr Éamon Ó Cuív (FF)	Galway West	aire@pobail.ie
Mr Jimmy Deenihan (FG)	Kerry North	jdeenihan@eircom.net
Mr Martin Ferris (SF)	Kerry North	martin.ferris@oireachtas.ie
Mr Thomas McEllistrim (FF)	Kerry North	tom.mcellistrim@oireachtas.ie
Mr Jackie Healy-Rae (I)	Kerry South	Jackie.Healy.Rae@oireachtas.ie
Mr John O'Donoghue (FF)	Kerry South	john.odonoghue@oireachtas.ie
Mr Tom Sheahan (FG)	Kerry South	tom.sheahan@oireachtas.ie
Ms Aíne Brady (FF)	Kildare North	aine.brady@oireachtas.ie
Mr Bernard Durkan (FG)	Kildare North	bernard.durkan@oireachtas.ie
Mr Michael Fitzpatrick (FF)	Kildare North	michael.fitzpatrick@oireachtas.ie
Mr Emmet Stagg (L)	Kildare North	emmet.stagg@oireachtas.ie
Mr Seán Ó Fearghaíl (FF)	Kildare South	sean.ofearghail@oireachtas.ie

Mr Seán Power (FF)	Kildare South	sean.power@oireachtas.ie
Mr Jack Wall (L)	Kildare South	jack.wall@oireachtas.ie
Mr Brian Cowen (FF)	Laoighis–Offaly	taoiseach@taoiseach.gov.ie
Ms Olwyn Enright (FG)	Laoighis–Offaly	olwyn.enright@oireachtas.ie
Mr Charles Flanagan (FG)	Laoighis–Offaly	charles.flanagan@oireachtas.ie
Mr Sean Fleming (FF)	Laoighis–Offaly	sean.fleming@oireachtas.ie
Mr John Anthony Moloney (FF)	Laoighis–Offaly	john.moloney@oireachtas.ie
Mr Michael Noonan (FG)	Limerick East	michael.noonan@oireachtas.ie
Mr Willie O'Dea (FF)	Limerick East	minister@defence.irlgov.ie
Mr Kieran O'Donnell (FG)	Limerick East	kieran.odonnell@oireachtas.ie
Ms Jan O'Sullivan (L)	Limerick East	jan.osullivan@oireachtas.ie
Mr Peter Power (FF)	Limerick East	peter.power@oireachtas.ie
Mr Niall Collins (FF)	Limerick West	niall.collins@oireachtas.ie
Mr John Cregan (FF)	Limerick West	john.cregan@oireachtas.ie
Mr Dan Neville (FG)	Limerick West	daniel.neville@oireachtas.ie
Mr James Bannon (FG)	Longford–Westmeath	james.bannon@oireachtas.ie
Mr Peter Kelly (FF)	Longford–Westmeath	peter.kelly@oireachtas.ie
Ms Mary O'Rourke (FF)	Longford–Westmeath	mary.orourke@oireachtas.ie
Mr Willie Penrose (L)	Longford–Westmeath	willie.penrose@oireachtas.ie
Mr Dermot Ahern (FF)	Louth	minister@justice.ie
Mr Séamus Kirk (CC)	Louth	seamus.kirk@oireachtas.ie
Mr Arthur Morgan (SF)	Louth	arthur.morgan@oireachtas.ie
Mr Fergus O'Dowd (FG)	Louth	fergus.odowd@oireachtas.ie
Mr Dara Calleary (FF)	Mayo	dara.calleary@oireachtas.ie
Ms Beverley Flynn (FF)	Mayo	beverley.flynn@oireachtas.ie
Mr Enda Kenny (FG)	Mayo	enda.kenny@oireachtas.ie
Mr John O'Mahony (FG)	Mayo	john.omahony@oireachtas.ie
Mr Michael Ring (FG)	Mayo	michael.ring@oireachtas.ie
Mr Thomas Byrne (FF)	Meath East	thomas.byrne@oireachtas.ie

Mr Shane McEntee (FG)	Meath East	shane.mcentee@oireachtas.ie
Ms Mary Wallace (FF)	Meath East	mary_wallace@health.irlgov.ie
Mr Johnny Brady (FF)	Meath West	johnny.brady@oireachtas.ie
Mr Noel Dempsey (FF)	Meath West	minister@transport.ie
Mr Damien English (FG)	Meath West	damien.english@oireachtas.ie
Mr Frank Feighan (FG)	Roscommon-South Leitrim	frank.feighan@oireachtas.ie
Mr Michael Finneran (FF)	Roscommon-South Leitrim	michael.finneran@oireachtas.ie
Mr Denis Naughten (FG)	Roscommon-South Leitrim	denis.naughten@oireachtas.ie
Mr Jimmy Devins (FF)	Sligo-North Leitrim	jimmy.devins@oireachtas.ie
Mr John Perry (FG)	Sligo-North Leitrim	john.perry@oireachtas.ie
Mr Eamon Scanlon (FF)	Sligo-North Leitrim	eamon.scanlon@oireachtas.ie
Mr Noel J. Coonan (FG)	Tipperary North	noel.coonan@oireachtas.ie
Ms Máire Hoctor (FF)	Tipperary North	maire.hoctor@oireachtas.ie
Mr Michael Lowry (I)	Tipperary North	michael.lowry@oireachtas.ie
Mr Tom Hayes (FG)	Tipperary South	tom.hayes@oireachtas.ie
Dr Martin Mansergh (FF)	Tipperary South	martin.mansergh@oireachtas.ie
Mr Mattie McGrath (FF)	Tipperary South	mattie.mcgrath@oireachtas.ie
Mr Martin Cullen (FF)	Waterford	ministersoffice@dast.gov.ie
Mr John Deasy (FG)	Waterford	john.deasy@oireachtas.ie
Mr Michael Kennedy (FF)	Waterford	michael.kennedy@oireachtas.ie
Mr Brian O'Shea (L)	Waterford	boshea@eircom.net
Mr John Browne (FF)	Wexford	john.browne@oireachtas.ie
Mr Sean Connick (FF)	Wexford	sean.connick@oireachtas.ie
Mr Michael W. D'Arcy (FG)	Wexford	michael.darcy@oireachtas.ie
Mr Brendan Howlin (L)	Wexford	brendan.howlin@oireachtas.ie
Mr Paul Kehoe (FG)	Wexford	paul.kehoe@oireachtas.ie
Mr Joe Behan (I)	Wicklow	joe.behan@oireachtas.ie

Appendix II. How to contact all the members of the Dáil

Mr Andrew Doyle (FG)	Wicklow	andrew.doyle@oireachtas.ie
Ms Liz McManus (L)	Wicklow	liz.mcmanus@oireachtas.ie
Mr Dick Roche (FF)	Wicklow	dick.roche@oireachtas.ie
Mr Billy Godfrey Timmins (FG)	Wicklow	billy.timmins@oireachtas.ie

Senator name	Email
Ms Ivana Bacik (I)	Ivana.Bacik@oireachtas.ie
Mr Dan Boyle (G)	Dan.Boyle@oireachtas.ie
Mr Paul Bradford (FG)	Paul.Bradford@oireachtas.ie
Mr Martin Brady (FF)	Martin.Brady@oireachtas.ie
Mr Paddy Burke (FG)	Paddy.Burke@oireachtas.ie
Mr Larry Butler (FF)	Larry.Butler@oireachtas.ie
Mr Jerry Buttimer (FG)	Jerry.Buttimer@oireachtas.ie
Mr Peter Callanan (FF)	Peter.Callanan@oireachtas.ie
Mr Ivor Callely (FF)	Ivor.Callely@oireachtas.ie
Mr Ciaran Cannon (PD)	Ciaran.Cannon@oireachtas.ie
Mr John Carty (FF)	John.Carty@oireachtas.ie
Mr Donie (Daniel) Cassidy (FF)	Donie.Cassidy@oireachtas.ie
Mr Paudie Coffey (FG)	Paudie.Coffey@oireachtas.ie
Mr Paul Coghlan (FG)	Paul.Coghlan@oireachtas.ie
Ms Maria Corrigan (FF)	Maria.Corrigan@oireachtas.ie
Mr Maurice Cummins (FG)	Maurice.Cummins@oireachtas.ie
Mr Mark Daly (FF)	Mark.Daly@oireachtas.ie
Mr Pearse Doherty (SF)	Pearse.Doherty@oireachtas.ie
Mr Paschal Donohoe (FG)	Paschal.Donohoe@oireachtas.ie
Mr John Ellis (FF)	John.Ellis@oireachtas.ie
Ms Geraldine Feeney (FF)	Geraldine.Feeney@oireachtas.ie
Ms Frances Fitzgerald (FG)	Frances.Fitzgerald@oireachtas.ie
Mr Camillus Glynn (FF)	Camillus.Glynn@oireachtas.ie

Mr John Gerard Hanafin (FF)	John.Hanafin@oireachtas.ie
Mr Dominic Hannigan (L)	Dominic.Hannigan@oireachtas.ie
Mr Eoghan Harris (I)	Eoghan.Harris@oireachtas.ie
Ms Fidelma Healy Eames (FG)	Fidelma.Healy.Eames@oireachtas.ie
Ms Cecilia Keaveney (FF)	Cecilia.Keaveney@oireachtas.ie
Mr Terry Leyden (FF)	Terry.Leyden@oireachtas.ie
Mr Marc MacSharry (FF)	Marc.MacSharry@oireachtas.ie
Mr Michael McCarthy (L)	Michael.McCarthy@oireachtas.ie
Ms Lisa McDonald (FF)	Lisa.McDonald@oireachtas.ie
Ms Nicky McFadden (FG)	Nicky.McFadden@oireachtas.ie
Mr Pat Moylan (FF)	Pat.Moylan@oireachtas.ie
Mr Rónán Mullen (I)	Ronan.Mullen@oireachtas.ie
Mr David Norris (I)	David.Norris@oireachtas.ie
Mr Brian Ó Domhnaill (FF)	Brian.ODomhnaill@oireachtas.ie
Mr Labhrás Ó Murchú (FF)	Labhras.OMurchu@oireachtas.ie
Mr Francis O'Brien (FF)	Francis.OBrien@oireachtas.ie
Mr Denis O'Donovan (FF)	Denis.ODonovan@oireachtas.ie
Ms Fiona O'Malley (PD)	Fiona.OMalley@oireachtas.ie
Mr Joe O'Reilly (FG)	Joe.OReilly@oireachtas.ie
Ms Ann Ormonde (FF)	Ann.Ormonde@oireachtas.ie
Mr Ned O'Sullivan (FF)	Ned.OSullivan@oireachtas.ie
Mr Joseph John O'Toole (I)	jotoole@oireachtas.ie
Mr John Paul Phelan (FG)	JohnPaul.Phelan@oireachtas.ie
Mr Kieran Phelan (FF)	Kieran.Phelan@oireachtas.ie
Ms Phil Prendergast (L)	Phil.Prendergast@oireachtas.ie
Mr Feargal Quinn (I)	Feargal.Quinn@oireachtas.ie
Mr Eugene Regan (FG)	Eugene.Regan@oireachtas.ie
Mr Shane Ross (I)	Shane.Ross@oireachtas.ie
Mr Brendan Ryan (L)	Brendan.Ryan@oireachtas.ie
Dr Liam Twomey (FG)	Liam.Twomey@oireachtas.ie

Appendix II. How to contact all the members of the Dáil

Mr Jim Walsh (FF)   Jim.Walsh@oireachtas.ie

Mr Alex White (L)   Alex.White@oireachtas.ie

Ms Mary M. White (FF)   MaryM.White@oireachtas.ie

Mr Diarmuid Wilson (FF)   Diarmuid.Wilson@oireachtas.ie

Appendix III. Important sources and references

Over the course of the past few years, I've read lots of stuff in books, research papers and websites in my own journey to here. There's still tons of good stuff I haven't read and even if I had access to all the information, including the fascinating secrets on new inventions and patents, I still couldn't claim to be expert. There are a lot of people who are much more informed, experienced and technically qualified than I am. If you're the analytical type who requires much more proof before acting on what you've read here, I outline below just a few of the sources upon which I've relied to frame my own thinking and that can act as a starting point for you.

The International Energy Agency (www.iea.org) The executive summaries of IEA annual reports on global energy trends should be compulsory reading, as should its occasional press releases and alerts. The IEA's chief economist Fatih Birol is regularly interviewed in the media and is a frank and competent communicator.

Association for the Study of Peak Oil and Gas (www.aspo-ireland.org) ASPO's websites are equally important and provide a foil to the information produced by many big oil companies, the EIA, the Commission for Energy Regulation and the IEA. In particular, you should study the reports produced by the elder statesman of peak oil analysts, West Cork-based Dr Colin Campbell. The international version of ASPO is www.peakoil.net.

The Energy Watch Group (www.energywatchgroup.org) The EWG is an independent, German-based, scientific organisation that studies global energy markets and was founded by Hans-Josef

Fell, a German parliamentarian. The group produces well-presented reports on oil, coal, uranium and other supplies of energy.

The Oil Drum (www.theoildrum.com) Another peak oil website, this one run by the Institute for the Study of Energy and Our Future (ISEOF), a Colorado-based non-profit organisation. It combines scientific research, commentary, debate and analysis and also hosts a lively discussion board.

Sustainable Energy Ireland (www.sei.ie) SEI provides regular reports on matters relating to Irish electricity and dovetails with the Department of Communications, Energy and Natural Resources.

Spirit of Ireland (www.spiritofireland.org) The Spirit of Ireland website outlines the plan to develop high elevation hydro-storage dams fed by wind power and reports on continuing developments as the project gathers momentum.

ETF Securities (www.etfsecurities.com) ETF has a very wide range of exchange-traded commodities and funds covering many of the sectors mentioned in *Energise*. If you decide to invest in any of these, I suggest setting up an online account with **TD Waterhouse (www.tdwaterhouse.co.uk)** to avoid the high commission charges levied by domestic Irish stockbrokers and which are quite penal on small investments. You can also use the same service to target any of the stocks covered in *Energise*.

Stephen Leeb is a prolific New York-based author who, since 1986, has published six prescient books that have accurately predicted economic shifts, including the dotcom-bubble burst and the rising of oil prices. He holds a BA in economics, an MS in mathematics and a PhD in psychology and he edits a regular newsletter principally designed for US readers, *The Complete Investor*.

Jeff Rubin, a former chief economist at CIBC World Markets, links oil price spikes to four of the last five recessions and is author of *Why Your World Is About to Get a Whole Lot Smaller: Oil and the End of Globalisation*.

Jeremy Rifkin, founder and president of the Foundation on Economic Trends (FOET), is the author of several books including *The Hydrogen Economy* and *The End of Work*. Rifkin is a leading economist and activist seeking to shape public policy in the US and beyond. He has acted as advisor to many national governments and provides an optimistic, insightful and uplifting analysis of future trends.

Richard Heinberg, who has written three books on peak oil, is a recipient of the M. King Hubbert Award for Excellence in Energy Education and lectures on oil depletion and its impact on urban planning and agriculture.

Brian Hicks, founder of Angel Publishing, is managing editor of *Energy and Capital*, to which **Chris Nelder**, a self-taught and deeply knowledgeable energy expert, also contributes. They co-wrote *Profit From Peak* in 2008. Both are gifted researchers and writers.

James Howard Kunstler, author of nine novels and two non-fiction books, is best known for *The Long Emergency* (2006). Regarded by some as a doomsayer and by others as a realist, his novels explore the possible future after fossil fuels.

Acknowledgements

I'd like to thank Merrill Lynch and Davy Stockbrokers for providing research papers into energy efficiency and renewable energy respectively, and Bloxham Stockbrokers for stock-specific research. There have been many others who've sent me reading material and links in response to media interviews, too many to mention, but to all who share my deep concerns about energy, high inflation and scarcity pricing for natural resources, I'd like to say a really big thanks.

For the record, at the time of writing, both personally and through my pension fund, I hold small investments in a number of stocks mentioned in *Energise*. These comprise: Petrobras, Cameco, Sasol, Jinshan, Vestas, EnCana, Transocean, Fortum, Fugro, ETFS Leveraged Gold and Leveraged Silver.

Eddie Hobbs has written three personal finance books, each a best-seller in Ireland. He has presented multi-award-winning television series for the national broadcaster RTÉ, including *Show Me the Money* and the 2005 blockbuster *Rip Off Republic*, which attracted record-breaking Irish television audiences for factual programming. He edits Ireland's personal finance magazine *You & Your Money*, is a frequent contributor to Irish economic debates and writes a weekly column for the *Irish Daily Star* newspaper.

By profession, he runs an authorised financial advisor firm, FDM Ltd, and has been a consumer advocate since 1993 when he published his first report, *Endowment Mortgages: The Hometruth*, which helped bring half of the Irish mortgage sales market to a close. He is credited with forcing the Irish government to legislate for transparency on life and pension products by taking an action under competition law against an industry price-fixing agreement in the late 1990s.

He has acted as a director and finance spokesperson for the Consumers' Association of Ireland from 1993 to 2006 and as the government-appointed Director of the National Consumer Agency from 2005 to 2009. He is aged 47 and married with four children.